A BLACKLETTER STATEMENT OF FEDERAL ADMINISTRATIVE LAW

THIRD EDITION

Section of Administrative Law and Regulatory Practice
American Bar Association

ABA
AMERICAN BAR ASSOCIATION
Administrative Law and Regulatory Practice Section

Cover design by ABA Design

Library of Congress Cataloging-in-Publication Data

Names: Funk, William F., 1945- author. | American Bar Association. Section of Administrative Law and Regulatory Practice, issuing body.
Title: A blackletter statement of federal administrative law / prepared by the Section of Administrative Law and Regulatory Practice of the American Bar Association ; [William Funk, chief reporter].
Description: 3rd Edition. | Chicago : American Bar Association, Section of Administrative Law and Regulatory Practice, 2025. | Includes index.
Identifiers: LCCN 2025019956 (print) | LCCN 2025019957 (ebook) | ISBN 9781639056477 (paperback) | ISBN 9781639056484 (epub)
Subjects: LCSH: United States. Administrative Procedure Act. | Administrative procedure--United States.
Classification: LCC KF5407 .B53 2025 (print) | LCC KF5407 (ebook) | DDC 342.73/06--dc23/eng/20250424
LC record available at https://lccn.loc.gov/2025019956
LC ebook record available at https://lccn.loc.gov/2025019957

Printed in the United States of America.

29 28 27 26 25 5 4 3 2 1

TABLE OF CONTENTS

PREFACE

In 2001, the Administrative Law and Regulatory Practice Section of the American Bar Association published its first edition of A BLACKLETTER STATEMENT OF FEDERAL ADMINISTRATIVE LAW. It was, at the time, the first collaborative attempt to provide an authoritative statement summarizing then-current federal administrative law. The Section enlisted a broad corps of the leading lights in the field to produce a document whose strength, then-Section Chair Ron Levin noted in his preface, lies in the way it "encapsulates the *collective views* of a wide segment of administrative lawyers and scholars." Moreover, its actual text was reviewed and approved by the Council of the Section. It was not the work of a few professors.

The Administrative Procedure Act is, of course, the heart of federal administrative law and has not been significantly amended since the first Blackletter edition, and the Constitution's text remains unaltered. Nevertheless, courts both Supreme and otherwise have interpreted their texts and put substance into their open spaces in ways that result in change to the law in effect. Thus, in 2013, the Section, using the same collaborative process, published a second edition to bring the Blackletter up to date.

Recent years have resulted in some major changes, not the least of which was the overruling of *Chevron*. So, again it was time to produce a new edition. This edition states the current law as of February 28, 2025. The Trump administration's initial flurry of Executive Orders and their downstream consequences may result in changes to what appears here, especially in the parts on the open government statutes and government management of the administrative process.

Like previous editions, this edition sets out legal propositions, in most cases without citation or reference to their source. We have included references to basic APA provisions. Citations to cases are infrequent. The effort is to keep the text clean, crisp, and straightforward. Moreover, while the Blackletter Statement endeavors to be a descriptive statement of current law, it is also only a summary. For more detail and depth, as well as citations, persons are encouraged to refer to the "Guide" series published by the Section, which covers each of the sections of the Blackletter, other than FOIA, Sunshine, and Advisory Committees. A GUIDE TO FEDERAL AGENCY ADJUDICATION, 3rd edition, is up to date. A GUIDE TO FEDERAL AGENCY RULEMAKING, 6th edition, is available and up to date on the procedures for rulemaking, and a seventh edition is currently in process. A GUIDE TO JUDICIAL AND POLITICAL REVIEW OF FEDERAL AGENCIES, 2nd edition, is available, but much has happened since its publication in 2015. A new edition of A GUIDE TO JUDICIAL REVIEW OF FEDERAL AGENCIES is in the works, and a new GUIDE TO EXECUTIVE CONTROL OF FEDERAL AGENCIES is on the horizon.

This edition of the Blackletter Restatement, like the last, owes a debt to the past Blackletters and their creators:

- Most notably, in the first edition, Paul Verkuil as the chief reporter; Michael Herz and John Duffy as his assistants; and reporters Michael Asimow, Peter Strauss, Tom McGarity, Ernie Gellhorn, Ricky Revesz, Hal Bruff, Cynthia Farina, Tom Susman, David Vladeck, and Bill Funk.
- In the second edition, Ron Levin and Michael Herz as Section chairs personally supervising the project, and reporters Michael Asimow, Jeff Lubbers, Richard Murphy, Kathryn Watts, Bill Funk, Bernard Bell, Kevin Stack, and Anne O'Connell.
- In this new edition, Bill Funk as chief reporter, and reporters Michael Asimow and Jeremy Graboyes for the chapter on adjudication; Jeffrey Lubbers for the chapter on informal rulemaking; Ronald Levin and Richard Murphy for the chapter on scope of review; Bill Funk for the chapter on availability of review; Bernard Bell for the chapter on FOIA, sunshine, and advisory committees; and Bill Funk and Jeffrey Lubbers for the chapter on government management of the administrative process.

Daniel Cohen
Chair, Administrative Law and Regulatory Practice Section

A BLACKLETTER STATEMENT OF FEDERAL ADMINISTRATIVE LAW

PREPARED BY THE SECTION OF ADMINISTRATIVE LAW AND REGULATORY PRACTICE OF THE AMERICAN BAR ASSOCIATION
APPROVED BY THE SECTION COUNCIL, JANUARY 25, 2025

CONTENTS

PART ONE

ADJUDICATION

PART ONE
ADJUDICATION

Under the federal Administrative Procedure Act (APA), 5 U.S.C. § 551, adjudication is any process for the formulation of an order, and an order is any agency action that is not a rule. As a practical matter, most people use the term "adjudication" to mean a decision by government officials made through an administrative process to resolve a claim or dispute between a private party and the government or between two private parties arising out of a government program. Adjudication is the agency process for issuing a legally binding order of particular applicability (including a license). This stands in contrast with rule-making, which is the agency process for issuing a rule that is, in most cases, generally applicable.

I. MATTERS SUBJECT TO ADMINISTRATIVE ADJUDICATION

Article II of the Constitution vests the "executive Power" of the United States in the President, and Article III of the Constitution vests the "judicial Power" in the federal courts. Questions sometimes arise regarding whether Congress may assign a class of disputes to an agency, or whether such disputes require the exercise of the judicial Power and thus must be decided by the federal courts. Disputes that involve "public rights" may be adjudicated by agencies, whereas disputes that involve "private rights" must be adjudicated by the federal courts. The line between public and private rights can be difficult to discern. As a general matter, however, public rights cases are those in which "the claim at issue derives from a federal regulatory scheme, or in which resolution of the claim by an expert Government agency is deemed essential to a limited regulatory objective within the agency's authority." Private rights, on the other hand, typically involve "the liability of one individual to another."

Separately, the Seventh Amendment to the Constitution "preserves" the right to a jury trial in "suits at common law." Because only federal courts can empanel juries, suits at common law must be tried in a federal court unless a party consents to adjudication in an alternative forum, such as an agency. In order to determine whether the Seventh Amendment grants parties the right to adjudication by a federal court, courts must consider whether the cause of action resembles common law causes of action, and whether the remedy is the sort that was traditionally obtained in a court of law. Under the first part of this test, courts compare the statutory action to 18th-century actions brought in the courts of England prior to the merger of the courts of law and equity. This includes actions at common law in 1791, when the Seventh Amendment was ratified, as well as analogous actions. Under the test's second, and more important part, courts "examine the remedy sought and determine whether it is legal or equitable in nature." Civil penalties are more likely to be found legal in nature than injunctive relief.

II. DUE PROCESS REQUIREMENTS FOR NOTICE AND HEARING

A. Basic Principles

The due process clauses of the Constitution's Fifth Amendment (applicable to the federal government) and the Fourteenth Amendment (applicable to state and local governments) require fair notice and an opportunity for a hearing when an agency takes an action of particular, rather than general, applicability that deprives a private party of a constitutionally protected liberty or property interest.

Due process analysis requires three determinations:

- A determination that a private party has a constitutionally protected liberty or property interest within the meaning of the due process clauses;

- A determination that a government action has "deprived" a private party of one of those interests; and
- A determination of what process is due in order to protect those interests.

B. Protected Interest

The due process clauses apply in cases when a private party has a constitutionally protected interest in "life, liberty, or property."

The term "property" includes traditional property interests (such as money or real or personal property) as well as "entitlements" (sometimes called "new property"). For an entitlement to constitute property within the meaning of the due process clauses, there must be a substantive standard that constrains the discretion of governmental decisionmakers. Examples of such entitlements include nondiscretionary government benefits and government employment (when employees are legally protected from dismissal without cause). These standards are established by federal or state law, including both statutory and contract law.

"Liberty" interests may be based on federal or state law, or on rights protected by the federal Constitution (such as freedom of speech). Liberty also includes freedom from bodily restraint and from governmentally imposed stigma that affects a person's or an organization's legal rights or status, as well as protection of such common-law privileges as the right as contract, marry, or engage in a common occupation.

C. Deprivation by a State Actor

To constitute a deprivation for due process purposes, government action must adversely affect a protected interest. Negligent actions, even if tortious, may not amount to a deprivation for due process purposes.

Due process attaches only to "state action." The action of an agency is state action. Questions sometimes arise regarding the actions of non-agency entities, for example government corporations and private entities subject to government regulation. The action of a regulated entity is not state action merely because the action is taken pursuant to government regulation. The action of a private entity will be considered to be state action only in limited circumstances, for example, when the private entity is performing a traditional, exclusive government function or acting jointly with the government.

D. Due Process

Determination of the procedures required by due process involves consideration of three factors:

- The strength of the private interest in receiving notice and a hearing (or a particular form of notice or hearing);
- The risk of error and the probable value of additional or substitute procedural safeguards to avoid error; and
- The strength of the government's interest in not providing notice and a hearing (or a particular form of notice or hearing).

These considerations govern both the adequacy and timing of the procedures required.

The requirements of due process vary with the particulars of the proceeding. In some circumstances, an individualized trial-type evidentiary hearing is required. In other cases, notice of the subjects of the agency proceeding and the opportunity to submit written or oral comments may be sufficient.

Normally, the hearing must precede the deprivation. However, the hearing can follow the deprivation in cases of emergency or in other situations determined by the three-factor balancing test.

III. THREE TYPES OF ADMINISTRATIVE ADJUDICATION

Procedurally, adjudication takes many forms. Some adjudications follow trial-like procedures (e.g., an evidentiary hearing), while others follow procedures that are more characteristically bureaucratic (e.g., an inspection, test, or election).

At the federal level, courts, scholars, and practitioners have developed different taxonomies for discussing adjudication. Traditionally, the term "formal adjudication" was used to refer to adjudications that involve, at some stage, an opportunity for a hearing as prescribed by the adjudication provisions of the APA (5 U.S.C. §§ 554, 556–557). The term "informal adjudication" was used to refer to adjudications not governed by these provisions. This distinction between formal and informal adjudication is misleading because many adjudications not governed by the APA's adjudication provisions are at least as formal as adjudications governed by those provisions.

Many scholars now divide federal administrative adjudication into three categories:

- **Type A Adjudication.** Scholars use the term "Type A adjudication" to refer to adjudications that involve, at some stage, an opportunity for a "formal" hearing as prescribed by the APA's adjudication provisions. Examples include the adjudication of unfair labor practice disputes by the National Labor Relations Board, applications for workers' compensation claims by the Department of Labor, and claims for Medicare coverage and payment for items and services to beneficiaries by the Department of Health and Human Services.
- **Type B Adjudication.** Scholars use the term "Type B adjudication" to refer to adjudications that occur when a regulation, a statute, or procedural due process requires an evidentiary hearing, but the APA's adjudication provisions do not apply. Examples include removal proceedings before the immigration courts, the adjudication of disputes regarding the patentability of an invention by the U.S. Patent and Trademark Office, and the adjudication of claims for disability compensation by the Department of Veterans Affairs.
- **Type C Adjudication.** Scholars use the term "Type C adjudication" to refer to adjudications that occur when no source of law requires an evidentiary hearing. Adjudication in such cases does not follow the judicial model and is more characteristically "administrative." Type C adjudications include a wide range of proceedings involving matters such as grants, benefits, loans, subsidies, permits,

licenses, immigration and naturalization, land use, foreign policy and national security determinations, and inspections.

For ease of discussion, we use these categories in the sections that follow.

A. Type A Adjudication

The APA's formal adjudication requirements apply in "every case of adjudication required by statute to be determined on the record after opportunity for an agency hearing."

Some statutes state explicitly that adjudication must be conducted according to the APA's adjudication provisions. Other statutes state explicitly that adjudication need not be conducted according to those provisions. Indeed, the APA itself states that the adjudication provisions do not apply when an agency decides a matter subject to a subsequent trial de novo in a court; the selection or tenure of an employee; proceedings in which decisions rest solely on inspections, tests, or elections; the conduct of military or foreign affairs functions; cases in which an agency is acting as an agent for a court; or the certification of worker representatives.

Other statutes are less clear. In such contexts, determining whether a statute that calls for a hearing (but does not use the words "on the record") triggers the formal adjudication requirements of the APA is a matter of statutory interpretation. As a general matter, mere reference to a "hearing" or "public hearing" is insufficient to trigger application of the APA's adjudication provisions.

B. Type B Adjudication

Statutes, procedural rules, or due process may require an agency to provide an evidentiary hearing. If no statute requires application of the APA's formal adjudication provisions, the applicable procedure is drawn instead from a specific statute or procedural rules adopted by the agency. These rules must provide for adequate notice and a trial-type hearing to satisfy any constitutional or statutory requirement for an evidentiary hearing.

In practice, the procedures of many Type B adjudications often closely resemble the procedures of many Type A adjudications. The main difference between them is the officer who presides over the evidentiary hearing: an administrative law judge (ALJ) in Type A adjudications or a different official in Type B adjudications (see Section VI).

C. Type C Adjudication

When no source of law requires an agency to provide an evidentiary hearing, the procedure required by agency regulations usually involves informal consultation between agency staff and the affected private party, exchange of documents, or oral argument. In cases where the adjudication involves the interests of other members of the public, statutes and agency regulations often provide for legislative-type public hearings.

IV. PROCEDURAL REQUIREMENTS

The procedures of administrative adjudicative derive principally from due process, generally applicable statutes (most notably the APA), agency- and program-specific statutes, and agency rules. Courts may not impose agency procedures not required by the Constitution, statute, or rule. Absent constitutional concerns, federal courts may not require agencies engaged in adjudication to add to the procedures required by applicable statutes and rules.

A. Type A Adjudication

Agencies that conduct Type A adjudications must follow the procedures set forth in the APA's adjudication provisions (5 U.S.C. §§ 554, 556–557), which provide a framework for conducting an evidentiary hearing.

1. *Pre-Hearing Procedures*

The APA requires agencies to give all interested parties an opportunity for a hearing only if the parties are unable to resolve a matter through informal methods or by consent. In practice, most cases are decided without the need for a hearing. For example, most benefits claims are decided without an evidentiary hearing, and most regulatory enforcement actions are settled. There is significant variation in the procedures that agencies use to resolve matters before a hearing takes place.

Even when a hearing is requested, there may be efforts to resolve the case without holding one. For example, section 556(c) authorizes presiding officers to "hold conferences for the settlement or simplification of the issues by consent of the parties or by use of alternative means of dispute resolution"; "inform the parties as to the availability of one or more alternative means of dispute resolution, and encourage use of such methods"; and "require the attendance at any conference . . . of at least one representative of each party who has authority to negotiate concerning resolution of issues in controversy." The Administrative Dispute Resolution Act, 5 U.S.C. §§ 571–584, encourages alternative dispute resolution and provides a framework for its use by agencies.

When a hearing does take place, section 554(b) requires that agencies provide notice of the hearing to persons who are legally entitled to such notice. The notice must specify the time, place, and nature of the hearing; the legal authority and jurisdiction under which the hearing is to be held; and the matters of fact and law asserted.

2. *Nature of the Hearing*

Hearings can take place in oral or written form. An oral hearing may be conducted in person or by telephone or video, so long as the form of the hearing provides adequate due process and complies with applicable statutory requirements.

Section 556(e) permits agencies to adopt procedures for submission of all or part of the evidence in written form in determining claims for money or benefits or applications for initial licenses "when a party will not be prejudiced thereby." Consistent with due process and statutory requirements, a written hearing (or summary decision) may be permitted in certain other circumstances, for example, when there is no disputed issue of material fact or when the sole dispute concerns a legislative fact or the interpretation of a statute or rule.

Although the APA does not state that hearings must be open, agency hearings generally must be open to the public. However, agencies may close hearings for reasons of confidentiality or to protect potential spectators, witnesses, or parties.

3. *Burden of Proof*

Section 556(d) requires that the burden of proof with respect to any decision rests with the proponent of that decision (unless otherwise provided by statute). The term "burden of proof" refers to the burden of persuasion. Unless a statute or rule specifies otherwise, the standard of proof is "preponderance of the evidence."

4. *Rules of Evidence*

Hearings need not conform to the Federal Rules of Evidence, and most do not. Section 556(d) requires that decisions be "supported by and in accordance with the reliable, probative, and substantial evidence." Presiding officers may consider and rely on evidence such as hearsay that would be inadmissible in federal courts. Agency adjudicators should "provide for the exclusion of irrelevant, immaterial, or unduly repetitious evidence." Agencies have power to prescribe their own rules of evidence, provided that those rules are consistent with due process.

Parties are entitled "to conduct such cross-examination as may be required for a full and true disclosure of the facts." The right to present oral evidence or to cross-examine does not apply when a hearing is conducted in written form, as described below.

Though agency adjudications are not governed by the Federal Rules of Evidence, the attorney-client privilege and like privileges may be asserted in an agency proceeding. Agencies may take official notice of facts not supported by record evidence. Where an agency has taken official notice of a material fact, parties to the proceeding are entitled to an opportunity to demonstrate the contrary.

5. *Record for Decisionmaking*

Under section 556(e), the transcript of the hearing, all papers and requests filed in the hearing, and matters subject to official notice constitute the exclusive record for decisionmaking.

6. *Decision*

Except in rare cases when an agency head serves as the presiding officer, the ALJ issues an initial or recommended decision. An initial decision becomes the final decision of the agency unless it is reviewed within a time provided by statute or rule. When a presiding officer issues a recommended decision, he or she certifies the entire record to the agency head for decision.

Under section 557(c)(1)(A) and (B), a decision must include agency findings and conclusions, and the reasons underlying those findings and conclusions, on all material issues of fact, law, or discretion presented on the record. An agency's departure from its prior decisions in a similar case must be disclosed and accompanied by an explanation for that departure.

7. *Administrative Review*

Most agencies have at least one level of internal administrative review. At many agencies, this review is conducted by the agency head. Many agencies have also established review boards or judicial officer positions to review ALJ decisions. Review boards are often staffed by "administrative appeals judges," who are not ALJs, or by members of the senior executive service.

As a constitutional matter, adjudication must be directed and supervised by one or more officials appointed by the President and confirmed by the Senate. This limits Congress's ability to insulate the decisions of agency adjudicators from review by a Senate-confirmed official, except perhaps when the adjudicators serve at the pleasure of the Senate-confirmed official.

Administrative review occurs most frequently upon appeal by a party. Administrative reviewers may also review initial decisions on their own motion. Except when a statute or rule guarantees parties the right to obtain review, review is typically discretionary.

An agency head, or another decisionmaker exercising delegated review authority, has all the powers that it would have in making the initial decision unless a statute or agency rule provides otherwise. Many agencies have adopted such rules. Absent such a provision, an agency owes no deference to an ALJ's initial decision unless that decision was based on the credibility or demeanor of a witness. Where the agency and ALJ disagree on the facts, the court will review the findings of the agency head, not the ALJ. However, the initial decision of an ALJ is part of the record for purposes of judicial review, and a reviewing court will take it into account in judging whether the agency's decision is adequately reasoned and supported by substantial evidence.

B. Type B and Type C Adjudication

There is wide variation in the procedures for Type B and Type C adjudications. These procedures derive from due process (if applicable, as discussed in Section II), statutes specific to a particular agency or program, and agency rules.

There are, however, several generally applicable federal statutes that do apply to all types of federal agency adjudication, including Type B and Type C. The most notable is the APA, specifically 5 U.S.C. § 555, which applies to all agency actions, and section 558, concerning the withdrawal of a license. These sections, discussed next, are most relevant in Type C adjudications given the relative dearth of procedures required by law.

There are also certain procedures common to Type B and Type C adjudication. One common feature is administrative review. In many Type B and Type C adjudications, a relevant statute or agency rule typically provides for review of an initial decision by a higher-level official, either an agency head or another employee.

1. *Right to Appear*

Under 5 U.S.C. § 555(b), "so far as the orderly conduct of public business permits, an interested person is entitled to appear before an agency or its responsible employees for the presentation, adjustment, or determination of an issue, request, or controversy in a proceeding[.]" This right to "appear" could be interpreted to provide a right to make an oral presentation to an agency (though not an evidentiary hearing) in a Type C dispute.

2. *Timeliness*

Under 5 U.S.C. § 555(b), an agency must "[w]ith due regard for the convenience and necessity of the parties or their representatives and within a reasonable time . . . proceed to conclude a matter presented to it."

3. *Statement of Reasons*

Under 5 U.S.C. § 555(e), the notice of denial of a written application, petition, or other request to an agency must contain "a brief statement of the grounds for denial" of the application. This requirement does not apply if the denial is self-explanatory or if it affirms a prior denial.

4. *Withdrawal of a License*

A "license" is broadly defined in 5 U.S.C. § 551(8) as "an agency permit, certificate, approval, registration, charter, membership, statutory exemption, or any other form of permission." Under section 558(c), the "withdrawal, suspension, revocation, or annulment of a license is lawful" only if the "licensee has been given notice by the agency in writing of the facts or conduct which may warrant the action" and an "opportunity to demonstrate or achieve compliance with all lawful requirements." These rights to receive notice and to remedy the problem do not apply in cases of willfulness or those in which the public health, interest, or safety require otherwise.

V. INTEGRITY OF THE DECISIONMAKING PROCESS

Depending on the context, due process, applicable statutes (including the APA), and agency rules can all govern the integrity of the decisionmaking process. Also relevant are federal ethics laws. All federal government employees are bound by a statutory and regulatory code of ethical conduct. The code identifies financial conflicts of interest that require a conflicted employee to be disqualified from participating in a particular matter, including adjudicatory decisionmaking. The regulations adopted by the Office of Government Ethics also create an aspirational standard: "Employees shall act impartially and not give preferential treatment to any private organization."

This section focuses on the integrity of the decisionmaking process in Type A adjudications but notes due process considerations, as relevant, which apply more broadly.

A. Bias or Prejudgment of Adjudicatory Decisionmakers

A decision by a biased decisionmaker may violate due process and, in Type A adjudications, 5 U.S.C. § 556(b), which provides that all employees participating in the decision shall do so "in an impartial manner." In such cases, recusal or disqualification of the adjudicator may be necessary. If a party fails to make a timely motion for disqualification, however, the party has waived the right to do so.

Under the rule of necessity, if disqualifying one or more decisionmakers would render the agency incapable of acting, those decisionmakers generally should not be disqualified.

Bias or prejudgment exists when the decisionmaker has a pecuniary or other personal interest in the case; has prejudged the facts against a party; or, prior to the commencement of the hearing, had developed personal animus against a party, witness, or counsel or a group to which they belong. Bias is not established merely because the decisionmaker has rejected the claims or the testimony of a party or because the decisionmaker has fixed views about law, policy, or factual propositions not related to specific parties.

B. Personal Responsibility of Decisionmakers

Under what is commonly referred to as the *Morgan I* decision (but not stated in the APA), an agency decisionmaker who did not hear the presentation of evidence must become personally familiar with the issues in the case prior to rendering a decision. The decisionmaker can comply with this requirement by reading portions of the transcript and briefs, hearing oral argument, reading a report of lower-level decisionmakers, reading summaries prepared by staff members, or receiving a briefing by staff members. An agency decisionmaker may also delegate the decision to a lower-level official if such delegation is permitted by law.

Agency decisionmakers are presumed to be personally familiar with the issues of a case prior to rendering their decision. Absent evidence suggesting the decisionmaker was not familiar with the issues, it is improper to conduct discovery on the extent to which a decisionmaker familiarized him or herself with the issues or the manner in which this occurred.

C. Prohibition on Ex Parte Communications

In the instance of a hearing in a Type A adjudication, 5 U.S.C. § 557(d) prohibits interested persons outside the agency from making, or causing to be made, ex parte (off-the-record) communications to an agency decisionmaker that is relevant to the merits. An "interested person" means a person whose interest in the matter is more specific than the general interest of a member of the public. The phrase "relevant to the merits of the proceeding" is broader than the term "fact in issue" (see 5 U.S.C. § 554(d)(1)), but requests for status reports are not "relevant to the merits."

The prohibition on ex parte communication in Type A adjudications covers agency heads (including individual members of the body comprising the agency), ALJs, and any "other employee who is or may reasonably be expected to be involved in the decisional process of the proceeding" (such as a staff advisor to agency decisionmakers).

5 U.S.C. § 557(d) applies only to communications from persons "outside the agency." Communications to decisionmakers from staff members inside the agency are covered by the provision on separation of functions discussed in Section V.E. The President is considered to be "outside the agency" even though the agency is located in the executive branch.

The prohibition on ex parte communication goes into effect at the earliest of the following times: (1) when the person responsible for the communication acquires knowledge that a hearing will be noticed; (2) when the proceeding is noticed for a hearing; or (3) at such time as the agency shall designate.

If a decisionmaker makes or receives a prohibited ex parte communication, he or she must place in the record the prohibited ex parte communication (if it was written) or a memorandum stating the substance of the communication (if it was oral). In addition, the decisionmaker shall place in the record all written responses, and memoranda stating the substance of all oral responses, to such communications.

Decisionmakers may, consistent with the interests of justice and the policy of underlying statutes, require a party who makes or causes to be made a prohibited communication to show cause why its claim or interest in the proceeding should not be dismissed, denied, disregarded, or otherwise adversely affected on account of such violation.

Decisions tainted by ex parte communications are voidable rather than void. A reviewing court must decide whether the agency's decisionmaking process makes the ultimate judgment of the agency unfair either to any party or to the public interest.

The APA section on ex parte communications does not constitute authority to withhold information from Congress. Nor does it extend to "disposition of ex parte matters authorized by law."

D. Legislative Interference with Adjudication

Legislative pressure on adjudicators may violate the APA prohibition on ex parte contacts and may also deprive parties of their constitutional rights to due process. Claims of such violations are most likely to succeed where the congressional pressure probably influenced the decision of the adjudicators, the communication concerned disputed facts as opposed to issues of law or policy, and the particular application of pressure served no legitimate purpose such as statutory revision or congressional oversight of administration.

E. Separation of Functions: General Rule

Under 5 U.S.C. § 554(d), an agency staff member who personally and significantly has engaged in an adversary function (i.e., investigation, prosecution, advocacy) in a case may not participate or advise in the adjudication of that case or a factually related case. Separation of functions does not apply in determining applications for initial licenses or to proceedings involving the validity or application of rates, facilities, or practices of public utilities or carriers.

The requirement of separation of functions prohibits ex parte advice to agency heads from staff members who engaged in adversary functions in the same case or a factually related case. But it does not prohibit advice to the agency heads from staff members who did not engage in an adversary function. Nor does separation of functions prohibit agency heads from personally engaging in an adversary function (such as approval of a prosecution decision) and later participating in an adjudicatory decision in the same or a factually related case. However, the individual must be an agency head both at the time of investigation and decision.

F. Separation of Functions and Administrative Law Judges

Under 5 U.S.C. § 554(d)(1), an ALJ is not permitted to consult off the record with any person or party concerning a fact in issue. Additionally, under section 554(d)(2), an ALJ may not be responsible to or subject to the supervision or direction of an agency staff member who is contemporaneously performing investigative or prosecutorial functions.

VI. ADJUDICATORS

A. Type A Adjudication: Administrative Law Judges

Unless a statute prescribes otherwise, the presiding officer in a Type A hearing must be an agency head, one or more members of the body which comprises the agency, or one or more ALJs. In practice, a single ALJ almost always serves as the presiding officer.

1. *Appointment and Qualifications*

At the federal level, ALJs are appointed by "[e]ach agency." Because ALJs are "inferior officers" under Article II, Section 2, of the Constitution, the appointing agency is interpreted to mean the "Head" of a "Department," as those terms are used in Article II, Section 2. A "Department" is any freestanding component of the executive branch, not subordinate to or contained within any other such component. When the powers of a multimember agency are vested in its members jointly rather than in its chair alone, the "Head" is the agency as a whole.

Under Executive Order 13,843, agency heads have broad discretion to adopt regulations and practices governing the appointment of ALJs. However, an ALJ must possess a professional license to practice law and be authorized to practice law when he or she applies for and is appointed to an ALJ position. Agencies must also follow the principle of veteran preference as far as administratively feasible.

2. *Powers and Duties*

The APA confers substantial powers on ALJs in the course of presiding at hearings, including the powers to issue subpoenas and take depositions as authorized by law, administer oaths, receive relevant evidence, and regulate the course of the hearing. These powers arise from the APA without the necessity of express agency delegation, and agencies are "without power to withhold [them]." They must be exercised subject to the published rules of the agency.

ALJs must be assigned to cases in rotation so far as practicable. The phrase "so far as practicable" permits a practice of categorizing cases according to level of difficulty and assigning ALJs in rotation among the categories in which they are qualified. The assignment of ALJs cannot be made with the intent or effect of interfering with ALJ independence or otherwise depriving a party of a fair hearing.

ALJs may not perform duties inconsistent with their duties and responsibilities as ALJs.

3. *Compensation*

Compensation of administrative law judges is set by the Office of Personnel Management (OPM) at designated levels independent of agency recommendations and ratings.

4. *Performance Evaluation, Incentives, and Discipline*

An agency cannot conduct performance evaluations of ALJs. An agency may, however, introduce managerial programs to improve the quality of case decisions, so long as these programs do not interfere with ALJ decisional independence. Agencies may also set reasonable production goals for ALJs.

An agency may not grant a monetary or honorary award or incentives to an ALJ. An agency may discipline an ALJ or remove him or her from office only for good cause. The good cause determination is made by the Merit Systems Protection Board (MSPB) after a trial-type hearing before the MSPB. Actions by an ALJ that undermine confidence in the administrative adjudicatory process constitute good cause for disciplinary action.

B. Type B and Type C Adjudication

The officers who preside over evidentiary hearings in Type B adjudication are not ALJs. They are often referred to collectively as "administrative judges" (AJs). Some agencies use the general title "administrative judge" for presiding officers. Others have adopted specific titles, such as "immigration judge," "veterans law judge," and "administrative patent judge."

Many AJs are, like ALJs, "inferior officers" under Article II, Section 2, of the Constitution, and must be appointed by the President, a court of law, or a department head. In practice, most are appointed by a department head. AJs are generally subject to the same laws governing compensation, performance evaluation, incentives, and discipline as other members of the civil service, though some AJs are subject to alternative schemes.

There is significant variation in the appointment, powers and duties, compensation, performance evaluation, incentives, and discipline of decisionmakers in Type C adjudications, and it is difficult to make generalizations.

VII. REPRESENTATION

A. Representation in Agency Proceedings

5 U.S.C. § 555(b) provides that a "person compelled to appear in person before an agency or representative thereof is entitled to be accompanied, represented, and advised by counsel or, if permitted by the agency, by other qualified representative." The Administrative Practice Act, 5 U.S.C. § 500, provides parties the right to be represented by a lawyer who is in good standing of the bar of any U.S. state, territory, or possession. The Administrative Practice Act does not address

representation by nonlawyers, though many agencies permit qualified nonlawyers to represent parties in proceedings before them.

B. Costs and Fees

Under the Equal Access to Justice Act (EAJA), 5 U.S.C. § 504, parties who prevail against the federal government in certain adjudications are entitled to an award of attorney's fees and other expenses. Eligible parties include individuals with a net worth of no more than $2 million, small businesses, tax-exempt organizations, and certain other entities. Adjudications to which EAJA applies include adversarial Type A adjudications and adversary adjudications under the Contract Disputes Act, Program Fraud Civil Remedies Act, and Religious Freedom Restoration Act.

PART TWO

INFORMAL RULEMAKING

PART TWO
INFORMAL RULEMAKING

The following summarizes the procedural requirements that must precede the legally effective promulgation, amendment, or repeal of a rule by a federal agency, as imposed by the Administrative Procedure Act (APA), other procedural statutes, and judicial decisions. Certain additional requirements imposed by executive order (primarily E.O. 12,866 as amended or supplemented) are also included. Requirements stemming from executive orders are not judicially enforceable, may be and often are waived by the relevant executive office, and are particularly subject to change. Economic impact analysis has been required since the administration of President Carter in one form or another and is assumed to be required in the future.

I. APPLICABILITY

A. Definition of a Rule

A "rule" is an agency statement designed to implement, interpret, or prescribe law or policy or describing the organization, procedure, or practice requirements of an agency. Although the definition of "rule" in the APA refers to "an agency statement of general or particular applicability," "rule" is usually understood to refer to a pronouncement that is intended to address a class of situations, rather than a named individual. Certain particularized actions, such as rate-setting or the approval of a corporate reorganization, are explicitly included within the statutory definition. A rule may be prospective, retroactive, or both, but an agency normally may not issue a retroactive rule that is intended to have the force of law unless it has express authorization from Congress.

B. Distinction between Informal and Formal Rulemaking

The procedures described here apply to "informal" (also known as "notice-and-comment") rulemaking. "Formal rulemaking" requires additional trial-type procedures, not described here but essentially the same as those described for initial licensing in the discussion of adjudication. Unless a statute expressly provides for rulemaking "on the record after opportunity for a hearing," or Congress otherwise unequivocally requires formal rulemaking, the requirements for informal rulemaking apply.

Agencies engaged in informal rulemaking may provide additional procedures beyond those established by the APA, other applicable statutes, and the agency's own rules, but courts may not require them to do so.

C. Exemptions

The following types of rules are exempt from all the procedural requirements: rules relating to public property, loans, grants, benefits, and contracts; rules relating to agency management and personnel; and rules that involve a military or foreign affairs function of the United States. However, specific statutes sometimes override these exemptions and agencies may voluntarily comply with notice and comment requirements despite being exempt from them.

The following types of rules are subject to publication and petition requirements but are exempt from the other procedural requirements set out below: rules regarding agency organization, procedure, and practice; staff manuals; interpretive rules; and general statements of policy. Courts are regularly called upon to police agency invocation of these exemptions. Especially with respect to interpretive rules and policy statements (often lumped together as "guidance" documents), agencies must make sure they do not treat them as binding or seek to add new requirements without seeking public comment.

An agency may also dispense with notice and comment, and/or may make a rule effective immediately, when it finds it has good cause to do so and explains its finding and reasons at the time of publication. Under time pressure, agencies, after such a finding, sometimes adopt "interim final rules" that are both immediately effective and published with an invitation to comment and propose revisions; a subsequent agency action to revise or confirm that rule should treat such a rule as if it were also a notice of proposed rulemaking.

Failure to publish rules, either in the *Federal Register* or as described by 5 U.S.C. § 552(a)(2), denies to the agency any possibility of relying on it to the disadvantage of a private party, unless that party has had actual notice of the agency's position.

II. INITIATING RULEMAKING

A. Means to Initiate Rulemaking

An agency may commence a rulemaking on its own initiative, pursuant to statutory mandate, or in response to an outside petition or suggestions from other governmental actors. Any interested person has the right to petition for the issuance, amendment, or repeal of any rule. The denial of a petition, which is judicially reviewable, should be at least summarily explained.

B. Developing a Proposed Rule

In developing a proposed rule, an agency may be required to evaluate the rule's impacts and prepare appropriate written analyses of (1) overall economic costs and benefits; (2) the extent of new paperwork and information collection requirements; and of various impacts, including on (3) the human environment; (4) small businesses, organizations, and governments; (5) state, local, and tribal governments and the private sector; (6) families; (7) private property rights; (8) the civil justice system; (9) children's health and safety; (10) energy supply, distribution, and use; and (11) federalism. Requirements (1) through (5) are imposed by statute; requirements (6) through (10) were imposed exclusively by a series of executive orders. Requirement (1), although now also required by the Unfunded Mandates Reform Act, was first developed by executive orders—currently, E.O. 12,866, as amended. In practice, the administration of E.O. 12,866, as amended, dominates executive branch implementation of all these requirements. Under that executive order, prior to issuing a Notice of Proposed Rulemaking, executive agencies proposing an economically significant rule (primarily those having an annual effect on the economy in excess of $100 million) must provide the Office of Information and Regulatory Affairs (OIRA), in the Office of Management and Budget (OMB), with an assessment of the proposal's costs and benefits. This analysis may, and typically does, incorporate the analyses required by other statutes and executive orders.

In addition, President Trump's Executive Order 14,192 requires that, subject to exemptions and waivers granted by OMB, whenever an agency (defined as an executive department or executive agency not in a department) proposes or otherwise promulgates a new significant regulation, it shall identify at least ten existing regulations to be repealed. The new regulation's costs must be offset by the elimination of existing costs associated with at least ten prior regulations. Further, OMB must provide each agency with a total amount of incremental costs (akin to a "regulatory budget") that it will be allowed in issuing new regulations and repealing regulations for the next fiscal year.

Prior to issuing a Notice of Proposed Rulemaking, an agency may issue and take comments on an Advanced Notice of Proposed Rulemaking and/or establish a negotiated rulemaking committee to negotiate and develop a proposed rule. Under the Negotiated Rulemaking Act, agencies are encouraged to explore the development of consensus proposals for rulemaking with balanced, representative committees under the guidance of a convenor specially appointed for that purpose. Such proposals, if generated, serve as proposed rules under the normal procedure.

Under the Paperwork Reduction Act, all agencies must obtain OIRA clearance of proposed informational collection requirements, including those put in place by rulemaking.

C. Semi-Annual Agenda

Under E.O. 12,866, all rulemaking agencies must prepare a semiannual Unified Agenda of Federal Regulatory and Deregulatory Actions under development or consideration. These are now published on OMB's website, reginfo.gov. The fall Agenda must include a Regulatory Plan, also published in the *Federal Register*, that identifies and justifies the most important "significant regulatory actions" the agency expects to issue in proposed or final form in the upcoming fiscal year and that must be submitted to OIRA by June 1 each year. E.O. 14,192 stipulates that no regulation may be added to or removed from the Unified Regulatory Agenda without the approval of the director, and that unless a regulation is included in the most recent version or update of the published Unified Agenda it may not be issued without the written approval of the OMB director. The Regulatory Flexibility Act also requires that agencies publish in the *Federal Register* semiannual regulatory flexibility agendas that identify those rules that may have a significant economic impact on a substantial number of small entities.

III. NOTICE OF PROPOSED RULEMAKING AND OPPORTUNITY FOR COMMENT

A. Requirements for a Notice of Proposed Rulemaking

An agency must publish in the *Federal Register* notice of its intent to promulgate, amend, or repeal a rule. Publication in the *Federal Register* is not necessary if all persons who will be subject to the rule, if adopted, are named and have actual notice.

The Notice of Proposed Rulemaking must include (1) a statement of the time, place, and nature of any public proceedings for consideration of the proposed rule; (2) a reference to the agency's statutory authority for the rule; (3) the proposed text of the rule, unless a description of the proposal or the subjects and issues involved will suffice to allow meaningful and informed public consideration and comment; and (4) the internet address of a summary of not more than 100 words of the proposed rule, in plain language, that shall be posted on regulations.gov. Caselaw has required the agency also to make available in time for comment thereon significant data and studies it knows to be relevant to the proposed rule, including any draft analyses previously made as under the preceding Section II.

B. Public Comment on Proposed Rule

After publication of a Notice of Proposed Rulemaking, a reasonable time (typically at least 30 days) must be allowed for written comments from the public. Executive orders have provided that such a comment period should normally be 60 days for significant rules. An agency may, but, unless specifically required to do so by a relevant statute, need not, provide interested persons the opportunity to present oral comments or cross-examine witnesses.

IV. THE RULEMAKING RECORD AND DECISIONMAKING PROCESS

A. Record Requirements

The agency must maintain, and allow and facilitate public examination of, a rulemaking file (often called a "docket") consisting of (1) all notices pertaining to the rulemaking; (2) copies or an index of written factual material, studies, and reports relied on or seriously consulted by agency personnel in formulating the proposed or final rule; (3) all written comments received by the agency; and (4) any other material specifically required by statute, executive order, or agency rule to be made public in connection with the rulemaking.

The notice-and-comment process and docketing practices have been transformed by the advent of electronic communications. Most agencies participate in the government's central rulemaking portal, regulations.gov, which provides a portal for the public to comment on any pending rulemaking, and also serves as the home for current and past rulemaking dockets. Comments sent directly to participating agencies are supposed to also be posted by the agency to the central portal as soon as feasible.

The obligation to disclose written factual material, studies, and reports relied on or seriously consulted by agency personnel is limited to materials whose disclosure would be required under the Freedom of Information Act. Thus, neither a summary nor a record of predecisional internal agency policy discussions, or like contacts with government officials outside the agency or private consultants, or confidential business information, need be included in the rulemaking file. Particular agency statutes or rules, however, may forbid or limit such outside communications or require that they be logged and made available to the public. The executive orders requiring economic impact analysis provoked concern about outside communications with OIRA, so E.O. 12,866 included transparency requirements.

B. Decisional Process

Again, subject to the obligation to disclose factual material, studies, and reports relied on or seriously consulted, the APA does not bar decisionmakers within an agency from freely consulting with other agency personnel, government officials outside the agency, and affected persons. Particular statutes or agency regulations may impose logging requirements or other restrictions. A decisionmaker will be disqualified for prejudgment only where the person's mind is unalterably closed.

Under E.O. 12,866 (and the other impact analysis requirements imposed by statute and/or executive order), a final analysis must be prepared in advance of the final rule; that analysis is generally a part of the rulemaking record. An executive agency may not publish a significant final rule until OIRA has completed, waived, or exceeded the time limit for its review of the rule under E.O. 12,866.

A rulemaking must be completed within a reasonable time, or within the time frame, if any, set by the relevant statute. If it is not, the agency does not forfeit its ability to issue the rule, but interested persons may seek court action to compel completion of the rulemaking.

V. THE FINAL RULE

A. Publication of Final Rule and the Basis and Purpose of the Rule

The agency must publish the operative text of the final rule in the *Federal Register* with an indication as to where it will be codified in the *Code of Federal Regulations*. The agency must also provide a statement of basis and purpose (usually called a preamble) that adequately explains the justifications, purposes, and legal authority for the rule and indicates compliance with applicable regulatory analysis requirements. The scope of this explanation depends on the importance and impact of the rule. The Administrative Procedure Act calls for only a "concise general statement of . . . basis and purpose." However, courts have required that agencies must consider and respond to significant comments received during the comment period. For rules likely to have significant economic or other impacts, the statement (1) must also demonstrate that the agency fully considered significant alternatives to its final rule and relevant information and scientific data, and (2) must explain the agency's rejection of any of the foregoing.

After a rule subject to OIRA review has been published, E.O. 12,866 provides that the agency and OIRA disclose specified information pertaining to the review.

If the final rule is not a "logical outgrowth" of the proposed rule, a second round of notice and comment is required.

B. Effective Date

A substantive rule of general applicability is unenforceable unless published in the *Federal Register* and ordinarily cannot become effective less than 30 days after its publication (unless it grants an exception or relieves a restriction).

According to the Congressional Review Act, no rule (with some exemptions but including guidance documents) can take effect until the agency submits a copy of it and a concise general statement about it to both houses of Congress and the comptroller general. "Major" rules with an economic impact of more than $100 million may not take effect until 60 days after publication or submission, in effect amending the APA. Because the act applies to all agencies, and it charges the OIRA administrator with determining what rules are major, OIRA requires independent agencies to submit for review any final rules that may be close to having that level of impact.

But the main importance of the act is that it provides an expedited process, if certain deadlines are met, for Congress to consider passing (and presenting to the President) a joint resolution of disapproval of a rule. If such a resolution is enacted, the rule is treated as if it never went into effect. The act also contains a carryover provision stipulating that a rule issued in the closing 60 legislative days of a session of Congress is treated as if it were issued on the fifteenth day of the next session. This has particular importance if it occurs during a change of party in the White House that coincides with control of Congress by the President's party.

PART THREE

SCOPE OF REVIEW

PART THREE
SCOPE OF REVIEW

I. GENERAL

Except where a statute provides otherwise, courts generally review agency action according to the principles set forth below. In applying these principles, a court should distinguish among the agency's legal, factual, and discretionary conclusions, because different standards of review apply to each category. The most influential statutory template governing scope of review of agency actions can be found at APA § 706, which this Part addresses. Some regulatory schemes are governed by statutes other than section 706 but are often construed as having the same meaning as the corresponding provisions of section 706.

II. STANDARDS OF REVIEW: STATUTORY ISSUES

A. In General: Independent Review

The opening language of APA § 706 provides that "[t]o the extent necessary to decision and when presented, the reviewing court shall decide all relevant questions of law, interpret constitutional and statutory provisions, and determine the meaning or applicability of the terms of an agency action." In *Loper Bright Enterprises v. Raimondo*, 144 S. Ct. 2244 (2024), the Supreme Court ruled that this language "incorporates the traditional understanding of the judicial function, under which courts must exercise independent judgment in determining the meaning of statutory provisions."

Loper Bright disapproved the prior, long-standing doctrine under which, in general, a reviewing court was required to accept an agency's interpretation of a statute that it administered unless the interpretation violated the clear meaning of the statute or was unreasonable. *Chevron U.S.A. Inc. v. NRDC*, 467 U.S. 837 (1984). *Loper Bright* discarded this doctrine, contending that *Chevron* "requires a court to *ignore*, not follow, 'the reading the court would have reached' had it exercised its independent judgment as required by the APA."

More particularly, the APA instructs courts to set aside an agency action "in excess of statutory jurisdiction, authority, or limitations, or short of statutory right." APA § 706(2)(C). This inquiry can include determining whether the agency took an action that the statute categorically forbids or failed to take an action that the statute categorically requires. It can also include determining whether the agency took account of factors that the statute forbade it to consider or failed to take account of factors that the statute required it to consider.

In resolving statutory issues, reviewing courts should rely on traditional tools of statutory construction. This begins with examination of the text. Depending on the circumstances and the statutory interpretation methodologies that the reviewing court prefers, other tools may include, where relevant, dictionary definitions, statutory structure, related statutes, traditional presumptions and canons of construction, legislative purpose, legislative history, judicial precedents, and established agency practice.

B. Delegations of Authority

A court's best, independent reading of a statute may lead it to conclude that the statute delegates discretionary authority to an agency. This delegation might, for example, take the form of express statutory language granting authority to an agency to define specified statutory terms. It might take the form of a grant of authority to fill up the details in a regulatory scheme. Or it might take the form of a grant of authority to regulate as "appropriate" or "reasonable." In such a case, the role of the reviewing court is to independently identify and respect such delegations of authority, police the outer statutory boundaries of those delegations, and ensure that agencies engaged in "reasoned decision-making" within those boundaries (see Section V). The court might find, using its independent judgment, that the statute does confer some discretion but nevertheless rules out the particular interpretation adopted by the agency, or a premise on which it relied.

C. Respect for Administrative Interpretations

As courts construe statutes in the exercise of their independent judgment, they are expected to show due respect for the views of the executive branch. *Loper Bright* confirms that this practice remains good law. In a classic statement of this practice, the Supreme Court declared that administrative interpretations of statutes, "while not controlling upon the courts by reason of their authority, do constitute a body of experience and informed judgment to which courts and litigants may properly resort for guidance. The weight of such a judgment in a particular case will depend upon the thoroughness evident in its consideration, the validity of its reasoning, its consistency with earlier and later pronouncements, and all those factors which give it power to persuade, if lacking power to control." *Skidmore v. Swift & Co.*, 323 U.S. 134 (1944). The factors specifically mentioned in this formula are highly influential in judicial review, but the list is not exclusive. In particular circumstances, for example, courts may also give weight to an administrative interpretation because it rests on factual premises within the agency's expertise, or because the agency adopted it contemporaneously with the enactment of the statute.

Cases applying *Skidmore* and other precedents in which a court evaluates an agency's views for their "power to persuade" are quite diffuse. Some decisions appear to accord considerable weight to the views of the agency being reviewed, while others seem to give little or no weight to such views. Moreover, the practice of according respect to agency views is only one factor in the overall process of statutory interpretation, which is itself notoriously unpredictable.

D. Major Questions

The "major questions doctrine" instructs that "there are 'extraordinary cases' . . . in which the 'history and the breadth of the authority that [the agency] has asserted,' and the 'economic and political significance' of that assertion, provide a 'reason to hesitate before concluding that Congress' meant to confer" the regulatory authority claimed by an agency. *West Virginia v. EPA*, 597 U.S. 697, 721 (2022). In such a case, the agency's assertion of regulatory power requires clear congressional authorization. *Id.* at 723. Lacking such authorization, the agency's action is invalid.

The major questions doctrine has no precise definition, but the Court has usually deployed the doctrine upon finding that an agency's rules would have "vast economic and political significance." An agency decision is especially likely to raise a major question if the agency bases it on a long-neglected or rarely invoked statutory provision or seeks to act outside its primary field of expertise. The doctrine can apply to a spending program as well as to a coercive regulation.

III. STANDARDS OF REVIEW: NONSTATUTORY LEGAL ISSUES

A. Section 706 on Nonstatutory Legal Issues

The court will set aside an agency action if it finds that the action exceeds the authority granted, or violates limitations imposed, by

1. the Constitution;
2. an agency rule having the force of law (as opposed to, for example, internal operating procedures);
3. federal common law, in the rare cases in which it applies;
4. any other source of law that is binding upon the agency, including a consent decree or other judicial order, international law, and (to the extent applicable and enforceable by their terms) executive orders.

See APA §§ 706(2)(A) (requiring invalidation of agency action "not in accordance with law") and 706(2)(B) (requiring invalidation of agency action that is "contrary to constitutional right, power, privilege, or immunity").

B. Deference to Agency Regulatory Interpretations

The doctrine of *Auer* deference instructs courts to accept an agency's interpretation of its own regulation unless the agency's interpretation is "plainly erroneous or inconsistent with the regulation." *Auer v. Robbins*, 519 U.S. 452 (1997). For *Auer* deference to apply: (1) a regulation must be genuinely ambiguous after exhaustion of traditional tools of construction; (2) the agency's reading must be reasonable; (3) the regulation must represent the "official" or "authoritative" position of the agency; (4) the regulation must implicate agency expertise; (5) the regulation must represent the agency's "fair and considered judgment" rather than, for instance, a convenient litigating position; and (6) the regulation must not cause "unfair surprise" to regulated parties by upsetting reliance interests. *Kisor v. Wilkie*, 588 U.S. 558 (2019). Where *Auer* deference does not apply, courts should evaluate a regulatory interpretation according to its power to persuade. (See Section II.C.) It is unclear whether *Auer* deference, even as limited by *Kisor*, will survive the overruling of *Chevron* deference for agency statutory interpretations. (See Section II.A.)

IV. STANDARDS OF REVIEW: ISSUES OF FACT

The following standards apply when courts review agency findings regarding purely factual questions. These standards also commonly apply to agency findings that may be termed "factual" but embody a degree of normative judgment. Such findings present what are sometimes called questions of "ultimate fact" or of "application of law to fact," or "mixed questions of law and fact." In reviewing these findings, a court is likely to look exclusively to the standards expounded in this section if the meaning of the law is not in dispute. Where, however, the parties disagree about the meaning of relevant law, the reviewing court must resolve that dispute using the appropriate test for adjudicating issues of law (see Sections II, III); if the agency action survives that scrutiny, the court then applies the appropriate standard stated in this section.

A. Substantial Evidence Review

Substantial evidence review applies to facts determined in proceedings subject to the formal requirements of APA §§ 556 and 557 or otherwise reviewed on the record of an agency hearing provided by statute. APA § 706(2)(E).

"Substantial evidence" is such evidence as a reasonable mind might accept as adequate to support a conclusion. This level of review is somewhat less intense than that employed when appellate courts review trial court findings of fact for clear error.

A court conducting substantial evidence review should consider the entire record or those parts of it cited by the parties. APA § 706 (last sentence). The "record" includes facts found through the exercise of official notice. The decision and factual findings of the administrative law judge are considered part of the record. The reviewing court must consider not just those portions of the record that support the agency's findings but also those portions that detract from it.

Congress occasionally provides that rules adopted after ordinary notice-and-comment rulemaking are to be upheld if supported by substantial evidence in the record. See, e.g., 29 U.S.C. § 655(f) (OSHA rulemaking). However, courts have held that such review is indistinguishable from arbitrary and capricious review.

B. Trial De Novo

When the agency action resulted from a proceeding in which a statute or the Constitution requires that the facts shall be subject to trial de novo, the court makes its own, independent findings of fact and determines whether the agency action is warranted thereby. See APA § 706(2)(F). Trial de novo is available when a court reviews an agency's denial of a FOIA request, but it is otherwise rare.

C. Arbitrariness Review

1. For agency actions not subject to a formal record requirement, the default standard of review for fact determinations is arbitrariness review. APA § 706(2)(A). Arbitrariness review assesses whether a fact determination has reasonable support in the administrative record viewed as a whole.
2. For agency actions not subject to a formal record requirement, the "administrative record" consists of a file of materials that the agency maintains as the exclusive basis for its decision; or, if no such file is maintained, it consists of all unprivileged materials that were considered by the agency or its staff (or that were submitted by outside parties) in connection with the action under review. Where procedural law so provides, the record must also disclose oral communications between decisionmakers and outside parties.
3. The court may, upon a proper showing, allow discovery and other evidentiary proceedings in order to supervise the agency's compilation (but not the supplementation) of the administrative record.

D. Findings Not Specifically Supported by the Record

Notwithstanding the requirement of record support for agency findings in formal proceedings, an agency may, with notification to the parties and opportunity to rebut, rely on officially noticed facts in a proper case. APA § 556(e). In addition, in both formal and informal proceedings, an agency need not provide more support for predictive or other judgmental facts than it can fairly be expected to have gathered at the time of the action.

V. REVIEW OF THE EXERCISE OF AGENCY DISCRETION

The APA instructs courts to "hold unlawful and set aside agency action . . . found to be . . . arbitrary, capricious, an abuse of discretion, or otherwise not in accordance with law." APA § 706(2)(A). As applied to discretionary policy decisions, arbitrariness review examines an agency's explanation for its action for reasoned decisionmaking, which includes determining whether there is a rational connection between the facts found and the choice made.

In practice, the stringency of arbitrariness review varies according to the nature and magnitude of the agency action. Thus, a court will typically apply the criteria rigorously during judicial review of high-stakes rulemaking proceedings (a practice commonly termed "hard look" review), but more leniently when reviewing a routine, uncomplicated action. A court may not impose its own policy preferences on the agency.

Commonly applied bases for reversal include:

1. The agency relied on factors that may not be taken into account under, or ignored factors that must be taken into account under, any authoritative source of law. (The caselaw often describes this ground as an element of the arbitrary and capricious test, although it can also be understood as a component of the court's legal analysis. See Sections II, III.)
2. The action does not bear a reasonable relationship to statutory purposes or requirements.
3. The asserted or necessary factual premises of the action do not withstand scrutiny under the relevant standard of review (see Section IV).
4. The action is unsupported by any explanation or rests upon reasoning that is seriously flawed.
5. The agency failed, without adequate justification, to give reasonable consideration to an important aspect of the problems presented by the action.
6. The action, where inconsistent with prior agency policies or precedents, fails to display an awareness of the change in position, fails to explain a changed view of the facts, or fails to consider serious reliance interests that its prior policy engendered.

7. The agency failed, without an adequate justification, to consider or adopt an important alternative solution to the problem addressed in the action.
8. The agency failed to consider substantial arguments, or respond to relevant and significant comments, made by the participants in the proceeding that gave rise to the agency action.
9. The agency has imposed a sanction that is greatly out of proportion to the magnitude of the violation.
10. The action fails in other respects to rest upon reasoned decisionmaking.

VI. ANCILLARY ISSUES CONCERNING AGENCY EXPLANATIONS

In applying the standards of review, as just set forth, courts examine material portions of the agency's own proffered rationale. Courts normally will allow an agency to defend its action only on the basis of reasons articulated at the time of the agency decision and cannot supply their own rationale for discretionary agency conduct or speculate as to the conceivable purposes underlying the action. A court may deem an error in reasoning to be harmless error if the agency clearly would have reached the same result even if it had not made the error.

The court ascertains the agency's rationale as follows:

1. An explanation issued contemporaneously with an agency action is treated as containing the agency's actual rationale for taking the action, unless the party challenging the action impeaches the explanation with a strong showing of bad faith or improper behavior.
2. Where an agency action is not accompanied by a contemporaneous explanation, the court generally remands the matter to the agency to supply an explanation.

VII. PROCEDURAL ISSUES

The foregoing standards also apply to allegations that an agency violated procedural law in taking the action under review, see APA § 706(2)(D). The court presumes the procedural regularity of agency action, but a person may come forward with facts to prove the contrary. An action will not be set aside because of a procedural error that plainly did not influence the outcome of the agency proceeding. APA § 706 (final sentence).

VIII. AGENCY DELAY

A court will compel agency action unlawfully withheld or unreasonably delayed, APA § 706(1), though such a claim can proceed only where a plaintiff asserts that an agency failed to take a discrete action that it is *required* to take. An agency's delay in completing a pending action as to which there is no statutory deadline may not be held unlawful unless the delay is unreasonable in light of such considerations as the agency's need to set priorities among lawful objectives, the challenger's interest in prompt action, and any relevant indications of legislative intent. In considering such challenges, courts are deferential to agencies' allocations of their own limited resources.

IX. REMEDY

As noted in the foregoing sections, in general, a reviewing court will set aside agency action that does not meet the standards described, instead of mandating a specific disposition of its own design. When an agency's exercise of discretion cannot be upheld on the basis of the agency's rationale, or no rationale can be discerned, or if the agency so requests, the court will almost always remand the action so that the agency can provide further justification. When remanding, a court normally will vacate the agency's action, except in special circumstances. Such circumstances may exist where (1) the court discerns a substantial probability that the agency can cure its error on remand and (2) vacatur of the rule would be disruptive or would not serve the interests of the parties who prevailed against the agency in the proceeding.

PART FOUR

THE AVAILABILITY OF JUDICIAL REVIEW OF ADMINISTRATIVE ACTION

PART FOUR
THE AVAILABILITY OF JUDICIAL REVIEW OF ADMINISTRATIVE ACTION

I. OVERVIEW OF PREREQUISITES TO JUDICIAL REVIEW

A. Statutory Basis for Subject Matter Jurisdiction and Venue

The APA itself does not provide jurisdiction in suits seeking review of federal administrative action, but the federal-question statute, 28 U.S.C. § 1331, generally does. General federal-question jurisdiction in district court does not apply, however, where special jurisdictional statutes such as the Hobbs Act, 28 U.S.C. § 2342, provide exclusive jurisdiction for review of specified classes of cases in the courts of appeals. However, using factors identified in *Thunder Basin Coal Co. v. Reich*, 510 U.S. 200 (1994), district courts may exercise jurisdiction despite such special statutory jurisdictional statutes if preclusion would "foreclose all meaningful judicial review," if the claim is "wholly collateral to [the] statute's review provisions," and if the claim is "outside the agency's expertise." For example, a challenge to the constitutionality of administrative law judges that would hear the plaintiff's case in an administrative adjudication satisfied these factors.

Under the generally applicable venue statute, 28 U.S.C. § 1391(e), venue is proper for a suit against an officer, an agency, or the United States "in any judicial district in which: (1) a defendant in the action resides, or (2) the cause of action arose, or (3) any real property involved in the action is situated, or (4) the plaintiff resides if no real property is involved in the action." This is a default provision that may be superseded by venue provisions in a special jurisdictional statute.

B. Waiver of Sovereign Immunity

Section 702 of the APA waives sovereign immunity of the federal government for judicial review of agency action where the plaintiff is seeking relief other than money damages. This waiver applies regardless of whether a petitioner invokes the APA's cause of action or some other cause of action. It also permits a suit seeking a financial award that does not technically constitute "money damages."

A claimant seeking money damages from the federal government must invoke a waiver of sovereign immunity other than section 702. Examples of such waivers include (1) provisions in agency-enabling acts that authorize an agency to "sue and be sued"; (2) the Federal Tort Claims Act (FTCA), 28 U.S.C. §§ 1346(b), 2671–2680, which waives sovereign immunity for certain tort claims; and (3) the Tucker Act, 28 U.S.C. § 1491, which applies, most importantly, to contract and takings claims.

C. Official Immunity

A suit against an agency official in her official capacity is functionally identical to a suit against the government and is subject to the same principles of sovereign immunity.

A suit against an agency official in her personal capacity implicates a different set of immunity doctrines. As injunctive relief is generally available directly against the government under section 702 of the APA, the primary significance of personal-capacity suits is that they create a potential path for plaintiffs to seek money damages.

The Federal Employees Liability Reform and Tort Compensation Act of 1988 (Westfall Act) provides that federal officials are immune from common-law tort liability for actions taken within the scope of their employment. 28 U.S.C. § 2679(b)(1). Where the attorney general certifies that the defendant was acting within the scope of her employment, the United States is substituted as defendant. 28 U.S.C. § 2679(d)(1). Whether the United States has waived sovereign immunity is then determined according to the terms of the FTCA.

The Westfall Act does not immunize officials from constitutional torts or from claims that they have violated federal statutes that authorize a cause of action. Executive officials, however, are generally protected from suits for civil damages for such claims by the doctrine of "qualified immunity." This doctrine blocks claims for damages arising from an official's performance of discretionary functions so long as the official's conduct did not violate clearly established statutory or constitutional rights. A right is clearly established for the purpose of this test if a reasonable officer should have understood that her conduct was illegal given the particular facts she confronted. Courts have accorded absolute immunity to certain officials in light of their special functions. For instance, administrative law judges enjoy absolute immunity from damages liability allegedly arising from their judicial acts.

The President may not be sued under the APA, because the President is not an "agency" under the APA. The President has absolute immunity from civil suits for official actions. The President also has absolute immunity from criminal prosecution for actions within his exclusive constitutional power. For the President's other official actions, he has a presumptive immunity.

D. Cause of Action or Defense

Many specific statutes authorize judicial review of particular types of federal agency action. An agency's enabling act may, for instance, contain a set of provisions establishing parameters for review of rules issued pursuant to that act's authority. Review pursuant to such provisions is sometimes characterized as a "special statutory proceeding." Often, the jurisdictional provisions for a special statutory review proceeding assign subject matter jurisdiction to courts of appeals (especially the D.C. Circuit).

In the absence of a special statutory review scheme, parties may seek review under APA §§ 702–704, which provide a general cause of action for parties "adversely affected or aggrieved by agency action" for which "there is no other adequate remedy in court."

Where neither a specific statute nor the APA provides a cause of action, parties may obtain review by seeking various forms of relief, including equitable relief under a federal court's general equity jurisdiction, 28 U.S.C. § 1331, declaratory relief under the Declaratory Judgment Act, 28 U.S.C. § 2201, and mandamus under 28 U.S.C. § 1361. (These forms of review, as well as review sought under the APA without authorization by a more specific statute, are sometimes described as instances of "nonstatutory review." This usage is misleading, however, because almost all of these forms of review rest on a statutory foundation.)

In rare circumstances, a plaintiff may sue an agency official in her *personal* capacity for a constitutional tort in a "*Bivens* action." See *Bivens v. Six Unknown Named Agents of Federal Bureau of Narcotics*, 403 U.S. 388 (1971). The Supreme Court has narrowly defined the availability of the *Bivens* cause of action, and it is not available where Congress has provided an adequate statutory alternative.

Rather than challenge an agency action affirmatively, under many circumstances a party may instead raise the invalidity of an agency action as a defense in a subsequent enforcement proceeding based on that agency action. The existence of a prior, adequate, and exclusive opportunity for judicial review may, however, cut off this right to raise the invalidity of the agency action as a defense in an enforcement proceeding. Cf. Section II.D.

E. Reviewability

Doctrines of reviewability block judicial review of certain types of claims that would otherwise appear to fall within the scope of the APA's general cause of action. More particularly: (1) the APA's cause of action applies only to challenges to "agency action"—and not everything an agency does satisfies the APA's technical meaning of this phrase; (2) Congress may by statute preclude review of certain types of agency action; and (3) courts regard some agency actions as unreviewable because they are "committed to agency discretion by law." See Section III.

F. Timing Doctrines

A complex set of timing doctrines limits access to the courts for judicial review of agency action. These include the following:

- **Finality:** In general, courts will review only final agency actions. Agency action is final if it (1) is consummated and (2) determines rights or obligations or otherwise carries legal consequences.
- **Exhaustion:** Parties generally must pursue available intra-agency remedies, such as an appeal to higher agency authorities, before seeking judicial review.
- **Ripeness:** Courts will normally not review a matter that is not "ripe," meaning that the issues raised in the case must be "fit" for review, and delaying review must cause hardship to the plaintiff.
- **Statutory deadlines:** The statute of limitations for cases brought under the Administrative Procedure Act is six years after the right of action first accrues. 28 U.S.C. § 2401(a). Other statutes may limit the time period for petitioning for review of agency actions to a period after the final agency action. In any case, courts generally construe such statutes to mean that even after the deadline has passed, the defendant in an enforcement proceeding may challenge a rule on the grounds that it is unconstitutional or exceeds the agency's statutory authority.
- **Primary jurisdiction:** Courts sometimes invoke this doctrine to stay proceedings that fall within their original jurisdiction, so as to permit an agency to examine an issue that falls within its special competence but that it has not yet addressed.

For further discussion of these timing doctrines, see Section II.

G. Standing—Constitutional, Prudential, and Statutory

The term "standing" covers three quite different concepts. First, for a challenge to administrative action to proceed in federal court, at least one plaintiff must demonstrate *constitutional standing*. To do so, a plaintiff must show that she has suffered an "injury in fact"—a legally cognizable injury. She must also show that this injury is fairly traceable to the defendant's conduct and that a favorable court order would likely redress it. Second, in certain circumstances, judge-made *prudential standing* doctrines deny standing to a plaintiff who satisfies constitutional standing requirements, as, for example, when the plaintiff sues to protect the rights of a third party rather than her own. Third, the doctrine of *statutory standing* inquires whether a statute authorizes a particular type of plaintiff to seek judicial review of agency action. Most important, a litigant may invoke the APA's cause of action under section 702 only if she is "suffering legal wrong because of agency action or [is] adversely affected or aggrieved by agency action within the meaning of the relevant statute."

For further discussion of these standing doctrines, see Section IV.

II. TIMING OF JUDICIAL REVIEW

A. Finality

Administrative law presumes that judicial review should await final agency action; interlocutory review is generally unavailable. The APA codifies this presumption at section 704, which provides, "[a]gency action made reviewable by statute and final agency action for which there is no adequate remedy in a court are subject to judicial review."

Agency action is "final" for APA purposes if two conditions are met. First, the action must not be tentative or interlocutory, but rather the "consummation" of the agency's decisionmaking. Issuance of an administrative complaint, for example, does not satisfy this first condition.

Second, the action must determine rights or obligations or create legal consequences. This condition implicates the following problem: certain types of agency rules—interpretive rules and policy statements—do not carry the force of law. It might seem that such rules cannot constitute "final agency action" because they do not carry legal consequences. In practice, however, interpretive rules and policy statements often have a significant impact on both regulated parties and the beneficiaries of regulation. This fact suggests that the finality requirement should not immunize these types of agency action from judicial review. Thus, agency actions have sometimes been deemed "final" for judicial review purposes where the decision appears binding as a practical matter—even if the agency has characterized the decision as nonbinding (e.g., by labeling it as "informal guidance").

Where an agency action is not final and no specific statute authorizes interlocutory review, a party may obtain review of the action in two ways. First, the party may be able to seek so-called nonstatutory review outside of the APA, but only if the agency action is clearly in excess of the agency's delegated powers or the ongoing action plainly cannot result in a valid agency order. Otherwise, the party may obtain review of all preliminary, procedural, or intermediate agency action or rulings on review of the final agency action.

B. Exhaustion of Administrative Remedies

An agency action may be considered "final" even though opportunities remain for seeking further review of the action within the agency itself. Nonetheless, where the *exhaustion* doctrine applies, it requires a plaintiff to seek relief from all available and adequate administrative remedies, including intra-agency appellate remedies, prior to seeking judicial review.

In some contexts, Congress specifies exhaustion requirements by statute, including the APA. Where Congress has not done so, courts determine whether to require exhaustion by balancing the needs of the reviewing court for judicial economy and an adequate record, the needs of the agency for autonomy and for a fair opportunity to apply its expertise, and the hardship to the plaintiff of denying review. The ordinary litigation cost of exhausting the administrative remedy is not sufficient hardship to render that remedy inadequate.

The Supreme Court has identified several sets of circumstances in which a plaintiff's interest in prompt judicial review strongly favors excusing exhaustion. These include (1) where requiring exhaustion would cause undue prejudice, perhaps due to unreasonable deadlines for administrative review; (2) where the agency lacks authority to grant effective relief; and (3) where the administrative body is biased or has predetermined the issue.

Section 704 of the APA carves out an exception to the courts' "common-law" authority to impose an exhaustion requirement on plaintiffs invoking the APA's cause of action. Unless expressly required by statute, a party seeking review pursuant to the APA of otherwise final agency action need not pursue any process for agency reconsideration of its decision. However, an agency may require exhaustion of any intra-agency appeals, provided (1) it imposes this requirement by rule and (2) it provides that the agency action is inoperative during the time of the appeal. In practice, most agencies do make use of this option when it is available.

In both APA and non-APA cases, the courts have frequently refused to consider issues that were not first raised before the agency. Courts enforce such *issue exhaustion* more stringently where the parties are expected to develop the issues in an adversarial proceeding than in circumstances in which they review the results of non-adversarial, informal hearings.

Some statutes require issue exhaustion in challenges to agency rules, and some courts have similarly required it even in the absence of a statutory requirement. Under this approach, a party that fails to raise an objection to a rule during notice and comment may not press that objection on direct judicial review of the rule unless (1) another party made the objection, (2) the agency's decision indicates that it did in fact consider the issue, or (3) the issue involves a key assumption that is foundational to the rule's existence.

Even where courts do not apply the issue-exhaustion doctrine, because the review of agency action under the "arbitrary and capricious" standard of section 706(2)(A) is limited to the record before the agency at the time of its decision, the agency's action may well be deemed reasonable in the absence of an argument that was not presented to the agency. Thus, the absence of an argument at the administrative level may affect the substance, if not the availability, of review.

C. Ripeness

To determine whether agency action is ripe for judicial review, courts balance (1) "the fitness of the issues for judicial decision" and (2) "the hardship to the parties of withholding court consideration." The Supreme Court has also advised courts to consider whether judicial intervention would unduly interfere with subsequent agency action.

The *fitness* inquiry largely turns on whether delaying judicial review until a rule has been applied to a particular, concrete situation could develop a factual record that would aid judicial resolution of the legality of the rule. Purely legal issues are thus typically, though not always, "fit" for review.

The *hardship* inquiry largely turns on whether a rule requires an immediate and costly change to a regulated party's "primary conduct"—that is, its day-to-day business. Thus, a rule requiring pharmaceutical firms to change their labeling practices or face possible civil and criminal penalties satisfied the hardship prong of ripeness. By contrast, a rule specifying that manufacturers of color additives must permit regulators to inspect their facilities on request did not.

Mere uncertainty on the challenger's part about the legality of a rule does not constitute hardship for the purpose of ripeness analysis.

Agency statements concerning how to implement or interpret a statute that the agency does not administer are unlikely to constitute hardship for the purpose of demonstrating ripeness.

D. Statutory Deadlines for Review of Rules

The statute of limitations for cases brought under the Administrative Procedure Act is six years after the right of action accrues. 28 U.S.C. § 2401(a). The right of action accrues when the plaintiff has a complete and present cause of action, which is when the plaintiff has the right to file suit and obtain relief. Because a plaintiff under the APA may not file suit until it suffers an injury from final agency action, the statute of limitations does not begin until the injury is suffered. However, other statutes may provide for short time limits (e.g., 60 days from the date of the final agency action) to petition for review. For example, the Hobbs Act sets a filing deadline of 60 days after the entry of the agency order. Similarly, the Clean Air Act generally requires petitions for review of most actions under that act to be filed within 60 days of notice of the action being published in the *Federal Register*. An agency may restart an expired statutory time limit on judicial review by "reopening" its consideration of an earlier action by either explicitly or implicitly undertaking to reexamine it.

Courts distinguish between "jurisdictional" deadlines and "claims processing" rules [the D.C. Circuit uses the terms "substantive" and "procedural"], the latter of which may be subject to waiver or equitable tolling. In order for a deadline to be jurisdictional, Congress must clearly so indicate.

Even after a statutory deadline has run, courts permit parties defending against application of a rule in an enforcement proceeding to challenge the rule on the substantive grounds that it is unconstitutional or exceeds the agency's statutory authority.

In some cases, a party can avoid the statutory time limit for review of a rule by filing a petition for rulemaking to modify or rescind the rule. If the agency denies this rulemaking petition, the party may then seek review of this denial. Such review, however, is limited to issues considered in the denial decision.

E. Primary Jurisdiction

Primary jurisdiction applies when claims properly cognizable in court contain one or more issues within the special competence of an administrative agency. In such cases, the court enables a referral to the agency, staying further proceedings so as to give the parties reasonable opportunity to seek an administrative ruling. In cases of mandatory primary jurisdiction, an agency ruling is required, and the court cannot proceed with the case until the agency has acted. In cases where an agency ruling is not required but the court might benefit from the expertise of the agency, the court may make a referral but also provide that if the agency has not ruled after a certain time the court will proceed without the agency ruling.

In determining whether to invoke the doctrine of primary jurisdiction, courts consider (1) whether the issues in a case implicate an agency's expertise or discretion, (2) whether the issues need a uniform resolution that the agency is best situated to provide, and (3) whether the referral to the administrative agency will impose undue delays or costs on the litigants.

III. REVIEWABILITY

A. "Agency Action" as a Limit on Review

The APA's cause of action applies only to "agency action." Section 551(13) defines "agency action" as including "the whole or a part of an agency rule, order, license, sanction, relief, or the equivalent or denial thereof, or failure to act." Given this expansive list, the APA's definition of "agency action" rarely blocks judicial review of an agency's affirmative action or its denial of a request for action (e.g., review of a rule or a denial of a petition for rulemaking).

The APA cause of action cannot be invoked to make a broad, programmatic attack on an agency's general work as opposed to an attack on a specific "agency action." For instance, an environmental group could not invoke the APA to challenge a Bureau of Land Management "program," although it could invoke the APA to challenge a specific agency action pursuant to that program, which, depending on the nature of the challenge, could have the effect of overturning the program.

The APA's inclusion of "failure to act" in the definition of "agency action" presents an interpretive challenge. At any given time, any given agency is failing to take an infinite number of actions—not all of which should count as "agency actions" subject to judicial review under the APA. The Supreme Court has solved this puzzle by holding that "failure to act" as used by section 551(13) includes only failures to take the "discrete" types of agency actions listed earlier in that subsection (e.g., failure to adopt a rule or to issue an order).

B. Statutory Preclusion or Limitation of Review

Section 701(a)(1) of the APA provides that Congress may by statute preclude judicial review under the APA. The Supreme Court has never decided whether the Constitution limits this preclusive power. Even if it did, plaintiffs in most cases would be able to sue directly under the Constitution. The Supreme Court has stated that there is a general presumption of judicial review under the APA. To overturn that presumption, the Court has said that either there must be "clear and convincing evidence of a contrary legislative intent" to overcome the general presumption of judicial review or the intent to preclude must be "fairly discernible in the statutory scheme." The Court has found implicit preclusion where judicial review on behalf of a particular group would "severely disrupt" a complex and delicate administrative scheme.

Where Congress restricts judicial review to particular courts or times by adopting special statutory review procedures, courts generally presume that Congress intends these procedures to be the exclusive means for review.

C. Matters Committed to Agency Discretion

Section 701(a)(2) of the APA recognizes that the APA's cause of action is not available "to the extent that . . . agency action is committed to agency discretion by law." This exception to the APA's general presumption of review is narrow. The Supreme Court has stated that this exception applies where statutes are written in such broad terms that there is, in effect, "no law to apply." The Court has also recognized that there are certain categories of administrative decision that are unreviewable as a matter of tradition. Functional inquiries regarding the desirability of judicial review also come into play—though not always expressly.

For example, agency decisions regarding how to allocate lump-sum appropriations are committed to agency discretion by law. In reaching this conclusion, the Supreme Court cited tradition and also noted that such allocations require complicated balancing of many factors and determining agency priorities—tasks best handled by agencies, not courts.

Likewise, agency decisions declining to initiate enforcement actions are presumptively committed to agency discretion by law. This presumption is based on judicial respect for prosecutorial discretion and for an agency's discretion in allocating its resources. Congress can, however, overcome this presumption by providing sufficient standards limiting agency enforcement discretion to guide review in a particular case. Also, where an agency refusal to initiate an enforcement action is based on statutory interpretation, the agency's inaction can usually be reviewed, at least if it is expressed in writing. (Notably, the presumption against review of nonenforcement does not apply to denial of a petition for rulemaking.)

Section 701(a)(2)'s exemption to review applies only "to the extent" that agency action is committed to agency discretion. As a result, some issues raised by an action may be reviewable while others are not. The Supreme Court has, for instance, held that a constitutional claim raised in connection with termination of a government employee was reviewable but that a statutory claim was not. Similarly, even where the substance of an agency's decision is committed to agency discretion, the procedure applicable to the action may not be.

D. Cause of Action

Section 702 of the APA provides the cause of action for review under the APA. It provides that "[a] person suffering legal wrong because of agency action, or adversely affected or aggrieved by agency action within the meaning of a relevant statute, is entitled to judicial review thereof." Although this language significantly broadened pre-APA availability of review to challenge agency action, it does not confer standing to the limits of what is constitutionally possible. In addition to showing that she has suffered a constitutionally cognizable injury caused by the agency's action, the plaintiff relying upon section 702 must show that her injury is "arguably within the zone of interests to be protected or regulated by the statute . . . in question."

Individual regulatory statutes may contain their own causes of action. Statutory language authorizing challenge by "any person aggrieved" has traditionally been interpreted to confer standing to the full extent of Article III, without regard to such prudential limitations as the zone-of-interests requirement. Citizen-suit provisions (e.g., those conferring standing on "any person" without further requirements) are usually given the same interpretation. Other kinds of statutory standing provisions are typically construed to incorporate the zone-of-interests test and other prudential requirements absent evidence of a different legislative intent.

IV. STANDING

A. Overview

The concept of "standing" determines whether a particular litigant is entitled to an adjudication of the particular claims asserted. Requirements imposed by the Constitution, the courts as a matter of judicial discretion, and Congress address this concept.

B. Constitutional Requirements

Article III's limitation of the judicial power to "cases" and "controversies" implies three standing requirements. First, the plaintiff must have suffered an "injury in fact"—an invasion of a legally protected interest that is (1) concrete and particularized and (2) actual or imminent, not conjectural or hypothetical. Second, there must be a causal connection between the conduct complained of and the injury—the injury has to be fairly traceable to the challenged action of the defendant, and not the result of the independent action of some third party not before the court. Third, it must be likely that the injury will be redressed or avoided by a favorable decision.

1. *Injury*

a. *The Constitutional Injury-in-Fact Requirement: In General*

The basic Article III requirement is "injury in fact." Constitutionally cognizable injuries include not only harms to person or property and economic harm but also harm to nonmonetary intangible interests. For example, so long as it is individually experienced, harm to environmental, recreational, or aesthetic interests can support standing. The injury must be actual or imminent, not conjectural or hypothetical. Mere ideological objection to government action does not constitute a constitutionally cognizable injury.

In addition to the kinds of harm that would have been recognized at common law, violations of some rights created by statute can also qualify as injury for purposes of standing. For example, violation of a statutory right to obtain certain information can constitute injury. However, not all rights created by statute can so qualify. For example, denial of a statutory right to comment on a proposed rule is not injury sufficient for standing.

The right of a prevailing party to claim a statutory bounty satisfies the injury-in-fact requirement; entitlement to attorney's fees or litigation costs does not.

The Supreme Court has suggested that when states are plaintiffs suing on their own behalf, as opposed to *parens patriae*, special concerns are involved that may lessen traditional standing requirements.

b. *Injury from Violation of Procedural Requirements*

When a challenged agency action harms an underlying substantive interest of the plaintiff, the plaintiff has standing to challenge the agency's failure to follow legally required procedures even though she cannot prove that the procedural error actually changed the substantive outcome. For example, a taxpayer whose tax liability is increased by a new regulation can challenge the adequacy of the notice of proposed rulemaking, even though it cannot be shown that adequate notice would have resulted in a more favorable regulation. However, she may be required to show that a more favorable regulation is possible. Cognizable injury cannot arise from a procedural violation without a showing that the action taken harms or endangers a concrete substantive interest of the plaintiff.

Apparently, the statutory right to attend meetings and otherwise have access to government proceedings, such as under the Government in the Sunshine Act and the Federal Advisory Committee Act, are sufficiently similar to substantive rights to be treated as such. FOIA rights and voter rights to certain information under the Federal Election Campaign Act are also substantive rights, denial of which will support standing without regard to proof of harm to a particular, underlying substantive interest.

c. Generalized Grievances Versus Harm to Informational Rights and Other Broadly Shared Interests

A "generalized grievance" is not injury sufficient to confer standing. Thus, harm to the general interest shared by all citizens in the government conforming its conduct to law is not a judicially cognizable injury. Accordingly, a statute purporting to allow "any person" to challenge agency action cannot authorize suit by a plaintiff without some distinct, constitutionally cognizable injury. However, a person who suffers a concrete, particularized harm does satisfy the injury requirement even though many other persons do or could suffer the same harm. Statutes can create and/or protect broadly shared interests, harm to which can constitutionally support standing. For example, individual voters can vindicate a concrete, though widely shared, right to election-finance information required by statute to be made public. Similarly, an individual denied access to government information or to an agency meeting has standing to challenge the denial, even though all citizens have an identical right of access. The widely shared injury, while satisfying constitutional standing requirements, may raise prudential standing concerns, but not with respect to suits under the APA.

d. Risk as Injury

The extent to which risk of harm can constitute injury for standing purposes is not clear. On the one hand, the Supreme Court has denied standing to an organization to sue on behalf of its members when it did not show that a *specific* member was threatened with an imminent concrete harm, even though it was virtually certain that *some* member would suffer a concrete harm in the foreseeable future. On the other hand, the Court found standing on behalf of organic alfalfa farmers to challenge the deregulation of genetically modified alfalfa because of the significant risk that the lack of regulation would lead to contamination of the farmers' crops. The fact that the farmers had already undertaken activities and expended funds to avoid the risk was apparently important to the Court's conclusion. In yet a third case, the Court dismissed a claim by persons challenging the constitutionality of a statute authorizing certain government electronic surveillance because it was not "certainly impending" that they would be subject to it, even though there was clearly a significant risk that they would be. The lower courts' decisions regarding risk as injury are in tension, with the D.C. Circuit holding that for increased risk to support standing there must be both (1) a substantial increase in the risk of harm and (2) a substantial probability of actual harm with that increase taken into account. Other circuits have generally been more receptive to considering any significant increase in risk of physical harm as sufficient cognizable injury.

e. Taxpayer Standing

In general, a taxpayer does not suffer cognizable injury because the federal government spends money in a manner objectionable to the taxpayer. The one limited exception involves federal appropriations for religious purposes. Although the doctrinal basis for this exception has been undermined over the years, the foundational decision has continually been distinguished rather than overruled.

2. *Causation and Redressability*

The constitutional requirements of *causation* and *redressability* ensure that there is at least a reasonable probability that the plaintiff's injury was caused by the defendant and will be remedied by the relief requested from the court.

Although stated as distinct requirements, causation and redressability are typically analyzed in tandem because it is rare that one exists without the other. However, if the court's remedial options are limited by statute or other law, the injury may indeed be traceable to the defendant's action, but not redressable by the available remedies. For example, a plaintiff who has suffered an environmental injury caused by the defendant will be denied standing on redressability grounds where the wrongdoing had ceased before the suit was filed, the plaintiff cannot demonstrate a reasonable likelihood that it will recur, and the only statutory remedies are prospective injunctive relief and civil penalties payable to the government.

Analysis of causation and redressability tends to be very fact specific, and in general there is no ready formula for predicting when a court will conclude that the causal chain has become too uncertain or attenuated. Cases attempting to challenge either favorable tax treatment of a third party or decisions not to prosecute appear to follow a pattern of dismissal on the basis of an absence of either causation or redressability.

Whether causation and redressability exist can be highly dependent upon how the injury is defined. For example, if the harm to a plaintiff challenging an affirmative-action program is defined as not obtaining the relevant position or contract, the plaintiff will rarely have standing, since almost never would a particular disappointed applicant be able to show it would have likely obtained the benefit but for the challenged program. However, the Court instead defines the injury in such cases as a lack of opportunity to compete for the desired outcome according to permissible criteria, a definition that eliminates problems of causation or redressability.

A similar definitional issue is posed by the suggestion, advanced by some judges, that complaints by regulatory beneficiaries categorically present difficult causation and redressability problems not faced by regulated entities. For example, it has been argued that consumers who can satisfy the particularized injury requirement and wish to challenge an agency's failure to adopt more rigorous fuel economy standards for automobiles must also show that if a more demanding rule were adopted, manufacturers would change their designs rather than pay noncompliance penalties. Because the standard for redressability is only that the favorable court decision would "likely" redress (or avoid) the injury, the plaintiff should have to show only that it is likely that the manufacturer will comply with the law.

Complaints about procedural violations provide another example. If the injury is defined as the actual agency decision, the plaintiff will normally not satisfy standard causation or redressability requirements, since it will be possible, even likely, that the agency could have reached, and on remand will reach, the same outcome even following proper procedures. The Court, however, has made clear that when the alleged violation is procedural, the normal standards for redressability do not apply. It suffices if the procedures exist to protect a concrete interest of the plaintiff and a favorable outcome on the merits will be possible if the correct procedures are followed.

Redressability issues can also arise under citizen suit provisions that provide only injunctive relief and payment of civil penalties to the government when the complained-of action has ceased after filing of the action, making an injunction inappropriate. While arguably paying civil penalties to the government does not redress the injury to the citizen plaintiff, the Court has said that such penalties deter future violations and therefore satisfy the redressability requirement.

A plaintiff need not show that its injury will be completely redressed or avoided to satisfy redressability requirements. For example, Massachusetts had standing to challenge EPA's failure to regulate mobile source pollution that contributed to global warming and rising seas, although regulating that pollution would not completely stop the rising seas. Similarly, the Court has also upheld redressability where only nominal damages were available.

C. Associational Standing

An association has standing in its own right if it satisfies the aforementioned constitutional tests. In addition, an association has standing to sue on behalf of its members when (1) one or more identified members would have standing to sue in their own right; (2) the interests it seeks to protect are germane to the organization's purpose; and (3) neither the claim asserted nor the relief requested requires the participation of individual members in the lawsuit. The second of these criteria is construed very leniently. The third effectively limits associations suing on behalf of their members to declaratory or injunctive relief, because if the redress required the payment of monetary damages, the persons to whom the damages would be paid would have to be parties themselves.

D. State Standing

The Supreme Court has said that a state is entitled to special solicitude in the standing analysis when it has a statutory right to challenge an agency action, and it is protecting its quasi-sovereign interests. Nonetheless, this does not relieve states' obligation to satisfy the three elements of standing: injury, causation, and redressability.

E. Prudential Standing Requirements

Historically, courts have referred to three judicially self-imposed "prudential" restrictions that can further limit standing beyond the constitutional minima. Congress may, by statute, override prudential restrictions on standing.

First, parties cannot raise claims or defenses that rest on a third party's legal rights (the *jus tertii* limitation). The *jus tertii* prohibition plays an important role in constitutional litigation but has not been very significant in limiting judicial review of agency action under the APA or specific organic statutes. A litigant attempting to challenge government action on grounds that it violates the constitutional rights of a third party may be prohibited from doing so unless (1) the third party has suffered an injury in fact; (2) the litigant and the third party stand in some close relationship; and (3) "some hindrance" impedes the third party's ability to assert her own rights.

Second, the plaintiff's interests must be within the "zone of interests" regulated or protected by the constitutional or statutory provision relied upon. In challenges to agency action, this requirement is subsumed under the APA requirement that the person bringing the suit must be suffering legal wrong or be adversely affected or aggrieved within the meaning of a relevant statute. This concept is more fully discussed in Section III.D.

Finally, the Court has sometimes stated that "generalized grievances" are precluded by prudential standing requirements. However, other cases have distinguished between "generalized grievances," which are not injuries for Article III purposes, and "widely shared" injuries, which can satisfy Article III's standing requirement, but which perhaps should be left to the political process to rectify. Whenever Congress has created a cause of action that allowed persons suffering generalized grievances to sue, the Court has always held that the limitation was constitutional rather than prudential.

The Court has, in recent years, criticized the concept of prudential standing. It has noted that such requirements are in tension with federal courts' virtually unflagging obligation to hear cases within its jurisdiction. In particular, it described the "zone of interests" test as simply a determination using traditional tools of statutory interpretation whether a plaintiff's claim is within a legislatively created cause of action. Moreover, the Court has come to settle on the preclusion of generalized grievances being based on Article III standing requirements.

PART FIVE

FREEDOM OF INFORMATION, SUNSHINE, ADVISORY COMMITTEES

PART FIVE
FREEDOM OF INFORMATION, SUNSHINE, ADVISORY COMMITTEES

I. THE FREEDOM OF INFORMATION ACT

A. Overview

The Freedom of Information Act (FOIA), 5 U.S.C. § 552, establishes a presumption that all records of governmental agencies are accessible to the public unless specifically exempted from disclosure by FOIA or another statute.

FOIA imposes the tripartite scheme of disclosure, as described next, as well as annual reporting requirements.

1. Federal Register *Publication Requirements*

Section 552(a)(1) requires agencies to publish in the *Federal Register* descriptions of agency organization, procedures for the public to obtain information, statements of agency function, rules of procedure, descriptions of agency forms, substantive rules of general applicability and statements of general policy, as well as any amendments to such material. Where a matter is required to be published in the *Federal Register* and the agency fails to do so, no person may in any manner be required to resort to, or be adversely affected by, the matter except to the extent that the person had actual and timely notice of it. However, matter reasonably available to the class of persons affected thereby is deemed published in the *Federal Register* when incorporated by reference therein with the approval of the director of the *Federal Register*.

2. *Public Availability Requirements*

Section 552(a)(2) requires that agencies make available for public inspection, in an electronic format, certain basic agency records that, while not subject to section 552(a)(1)'s publication requirement, are to be made available in agency reading rooms and (for records created on or after November 1, 1996) in "electronic" reading rooms accessible by computer. Four categories of records are subject to this disclosure requirement. The first three are (1) final opinions in agency adjudications, (2) statements of policy and interpretations not published in the *Federal Register*, and (3) administrative and staff manuals that affect the public. These three categories embody a strong aversion to "secret law" and ensure easy public access to "the information necessary to deal effectively and upon equal footing with the Federal agencies" represented. The categories thus reflect an affirmative congressional purpose to require disclosure of documents that have "the force and effect of law." Thus, for example, agencies typically construe "final opinions in agency adjudications" to include only those final adjudicatory opinions of precedential value. Subsections (a)(1) and (a)(2) both address "statements of policy and interpretation," and it remains unclear which must be published in the *Federal Register* and which need only be made available in the agency's electronic reading room. The fourth section 552(a)(2) category is records that the agency has already released to one requester, where the records either (1) have been requested three or more times or (2) due to their content, have or will likely be the subject of subsequent requests for substantially the same records. Material required to be made publicly available may be used by the agency only if indexed and made available or published, or if the party affected otherwise has timely notice of the materials.

3. *Records Disclosed on Request*

All other records, unless exempt from required disclosure under section 552(b) ("exemptions") or excluded from FOIA coverage under section 552(c) ("exclusions"), must be disclosed upon request.

Disclosure is to be effected pursuant to published agency rules. The bulk of FOIA litigation, and subsections B and C of this section, involves this provision.

4. *Annual Report Requirement*

Agencies must produce an annual FOIA report regarding compliance with and implementation of FOIA along 17 parameters. The report must provide information broken down by principal agency components as well as in the aggregate for the agency as a whole. The agency must make the report and the underlying raw statistical data available for public inspection in an electronic format without charge.

B. Mechanics of Operation

FOIA provides that any person, including corporations, associations, and foreign persons, entities and governments, may request agency records. However, a few exceptions have been carved out for fugitives, those who have waived FOIA rights in plea agreements, and foreign and international governmental entities seeking information from the intelligence community. Agency compliance is subject to the requester's willingness to pay applicable search, review, and copying fees, unless waived by the agency. FOIA imposes no "need to know" requirement, and thus an agency *must* disclose any requested information that is not exempted. Moreover, reflecting the core principle that information subject to disclosure "belongs to all," agencies cannot limit the requester's further dissemination of any records obtained. Requesters cannot require the government to create new documents, including explanations of preexisting documents, so agencies need not create new documents in response to FOIA requests.

1. *Definition of Agency*

FOIA applies to any "agency," which includes any executive department, military department, government corporation, government-controlled corporation, or other establishment in the executive branch of the government, including any independent regulatory agency. The definition includes the Executive Office of the President, but courts have held that components of the Executive Office of the President that function solely to advise and assist the President and do not wield substantial authority independent of the President are not covered. For example, while the Office of Management and Budget is covered, the Council of Economic Advisors and the Office of Administration are not. FOIA's definition of agency extends to entities that "perform governmental functions and control information of interest to the public" and includes entities that may not be considered agencies under the APA. Important factors in determining whether an entity is an agency subject to FOIA include whether the entity "has any authority in law to make decisions," has substantial independent authority in the exercise of its functions, and deals directly with those subject to its decisions.

2. *Application to Agency Records*

FOIA applies only to "agency records." Under the *DOJ v. Tax Analyst* test, agency records are materials that (1) are either created or obtained by an agency and (2) are in that agency's physical possession and under its control. FOIA provides that material maintained by an entity under a records-management contract with an agency, at the time of the FOIA request, are also agency records. In most cases, whether an agency has maintained "control" over a record sufficient to satisfy the second element of the *Tax Analyst* test depends on four factors: (1) the document creator's intent to retain or relinquish control over the record; (2) the agency's ability to use and dispose of the record as it sees fit; (3) the extent to which agency personnel have read or relied upon the document; and (4) the degree to which the document has been integrated into the agency's record systems or files. Generally, records not meeting the two *Tax Analyst* criteria, such as documents held by government contractors, are not agency records, even if subject to an agency's *right* of access. However, a nonprofit grantee's research data underlying published research findings produced under a grant and used in developing an agency action that has the force and effect of law are subject to FOIA. Some documents created and maintained by an agency employee, such as desk calendars, electronic calendars, and telephone logs, may be considered "personal papers" that do not qualify as agency records. As noted previously, FOIA does not compel government agencies to create records. In very rare circumstances, courts may require agencies to attempt to recreate destroyed records or to provide an explanation for records containing codes or notations that mask the records' meaning. Documents may not qualify as agency records, even though in the agency's possession, because they are held for or created by either Congress (or congressional committees) or the Office of the President. "Records" include information maintained in any format, including an electronic format. Moreover, the creation and use of a computer program to retrieve information stored digitally does not constitute creation of a new record.

A record includes any "item, collection, or grouping of information that pertains to the subject of a specific FOIA request." Thus, as a general matter, an agency may not redact a portion of a document merely because that portion of the document standing alone is not responsive to a FOIA request—the entire document must be produced unless the unresponsive part also falls within an exemption. However, in limited circumstances, an agency may consider a single communication or document as encompassing several distinct records, some of which are responsive and some of which are not. Diplomatic cables, which combine messages to different officials on different subjects for administrative convenience, are an example of such documents. In such circumstances, the agency may treat different portions of the document or communication as distinct records and produce only the responsive records. This practice has been referred to as "scoping."

3. *Specificity and Form of Request*

Requesters must "reasonably describe" records sought so as to "enable[] a professional employee of the agency who was familiar with the subject area of the request to locate the records with a reasonable amount of effort." Requesters must also comply with all published rules of the agency. FOIA does not prohibit a duplicate request for records after the agency has provided records in response to a prior request by the same requester. Thus, a requester may send a duplicate request to test whether the agency's initial production was complete.

4. *Fees and Fee Waivers*

Subject to some limitations, agencies may impose reasonable standard fees, in accordance with the agency's published fee schedules, for copying requested agency records. Agency fee schedules must be consistent with the Office of Management and Budget's *Uniform Freedom of Information Act Fee Schedule and Guidelines* (including the December 17, 2020, revision of the *Schedule and Guidelines*). Depending on the status of the requester—(1) commercial; (2) educational institutions, or noncommercial scientific institutions whose purpose is scholarly or scientific research, or a representative of the news media; or (3) other requesters—and the purpose of the request, agencies can charge reasonable standard fees for searching and reviewing records as well as for duplication. Commercial requesters may be charged for the search, review, and duplication of records. Educational institutions and qualifying noncommercial scientific institutions can be charged only the cost of duplication so long as the records are sought for scholarly or scientific research and not for commercial use. News media representatives also can be charged only for duplication costs. All other requests can be charged search and duplication costs. For requests from the aforementioned second and third categories of requesters, no fee shall be charged for the first 100 pages of document copying or for the first two hours of search time. Agencies may reduce or waive fees where the disclosure of information is likely to contribute significantly to public understanding of the government's activities and is not primarily in the requesters' commercial interest. Generally, agencies may not charge search fees for requesters that fall into categories one and three (or duplication fees for those who fall into the second category) if it fails to comply with statutory time limits for processing the request (which may be tolled for one additional ten-day period when the agency determines that "unusual circumstances" exist and provides timely written notice to the requester). If an agency has determined that unusual circumstances apply and that production of more than 5,000 pages of records is necessary to respond to the request, an agency may charge search fees (or, for requesters in the second category, duplication fees) if the agency has followed statutory procedures that give the requester an opportunity to limit the scope of the request.

5. *Time for Administrative Determination; Administrative Expedition*

An agency must ordinarily make its initial determination of whether and to what extent it will disclose records within 20 working days of a receipt of a request for information, and to make a determination on any appeal contesting its initial determination within 20 working days of receiving the appeal. In "unusual circumstances," an agency can extend these deadlines by an additional ten working days. The agency is required to notify the requester of "the determination and the reasons underlying it." The agency must also notify the requester of its right to "seek assistance from the FOIA Public Liaison of the agency." When the decision is adverse to the requester, the agency must inform the requester of the requester's right to appeal within a time frame determined by the head of the agency or "seek dispute resolution services from the agency's FOIA Public Liaison or the Office of Government Information Services." The deadline for appeal can be no less than 90 days from the date of the adverse determination.

A requester can seek expedited processing of a request upon a showing of "compelling need" or in other cases determined by the agency to be appropriate. A compelling need exists if failure to obtain the information on an expedited basis could reasonably be expected to pose an imminent threat to the life or physical safety of an individual (a term that probably does not encompass nonhuman animals). In addition, a compelling need exists if "a person primarily engaged in the dissemination of information," such as a journalist or a public interest group, can show an "urgency to inform the public concerning actual or alleged Federal government activity." An agency must act on a request for expedition within ten days of its receipt. Where an agency fails to comply with the statutory deadlines, the requester may treat the delay as a denial and either appeal administratively or litigate in federal court.

6. *Search Required*

An agency's search for requested records must be "reasonably calculated to recover all relevant documents." The agency cannot limit its search to only the initial locations where it believes responsive records might be held, but may need to expand the search to other locations reasonably likely to hold requested documents, based on "clear and certain" leads developed during its search suggesting the existence of documents it has not yet located. Requesters can also suggest potential search terms or locations where documents might be found, and an agency's unexplained failure to follow up on reasonable suggestions may undermine its defense of its search's adequacy. The adequacy of a FOIA search is generally determined by the appropriateness of the agency's search methodology, not by the search's fruits. The adequacy of an agency's search methodology is judged by a test of "reasonableness," which varies from case to case. Searches need not be perfect. Thus, an agency need not prove that it has located every responsive record, and the requester's production of a document the agency has failed to locate does not, by itself, establish the inadequacy of the agency's search. While agency employees are *often* presumed to have complied with applicable federal records laws regarding the professional use of personal email accounts, *the presumption is rebuttable.* Many FOIA cases involve challenges to the sufficiency of the agency's search, and the cases are far too fact-dependent to yield many meaningful and easily stated principles of law.

Agencies frequently establish a temporal limitation, or a "cutoff" date, such that records created after the cutoff date can be considered nonresponsive. Courts have generally approved this practice but review the agency's choice of the cutoff date for reasonableness (as a part of reviewing the adequacy of the search). Courts appear to favor cutoff dates based on the date of the agency's search rather than on some earlier date, such as the date of the request.

If a requester challenges the adequacy or thoroughness of an agency's search for records in district court, the agency bears the burden of proving the reasonableness of its efforts and must provide details of the procedures used in its search.

In adopting the E-FOIA Act, Congress contemplated that "[c]omputer records found in a database rather than in a file cabinet may require the application of codes or some form of programming to retrieve the information." Thus, searching electronic records or producing records in the form or format specified by the FOIA requester (see subsection I.B.8) may require agency manipulation of a database's contents. Such obligations can sometimes stand in tension with the principle that FOIA imposes no obligation upon agencies to create new documents. As several courts have observed, identifying when the manipulation of data points in an electronic database "crosses the all-important line" between searching a database and creating a record is not always an easy task.

7. *Segregation Requirement*

Where a requested record contains both exempt and nonexempt information, an agency must disclose nonexempt, reasonably segregable portions of the record and indicate the amount of information deleted and the exemption under which the deletion is made. Determinations of whether record portions are reasonably segregable are based on the intelligibility of the nonexempt material and the burden of editing or segregating it.

8. *Format*

FOIA directs agencies to (1) provide responsive records in any form or format requested if the record is readily reproducible by the agency in such form or format, and (2) make reasonable efforts to maintain its records in reproducible forms or formats.

9. "Still Interested" Inquiries

Given endemic delays in processing FOIA requests in many agencies, the passage of time or a change in circumstance may make the agency question whether a requester remains interested in obtaining requested records. In such circumstances, many agencies send the requester a "still interested letter." When done "judiciously," that is, when there is a reasonable basis for the inquiry and the inquiry is not made multiple times, and in accordance with Office of Information Policy guidance regarding the circumstances and manner of doing so, making such an inquiry is appropriate.

10. Administrative Appeal

A requester may appeal to the head of the agency of a denial of a request, an inadequate agency search for records, an agency failure to respond to a request within the statutory time limits, the imposition of excessive fees, or an agency denial of a request for waiver or reduction of fees. A requester may obtain expedited review upon a showing of "exceptional need or urgency."

11. Judicial Review

A requester may seek judicial review of each of the agency actions mentioned in the preceding paragraphs. See Section II.

C. Exemptions, the Foreseeable Harm Standard, and the Public Acknowledgement Doctrine

FOIA requires that all government records must be published or made available to the public unless they fall into one of the nine enumerated exemptions in section 552(b). The exemptions are to be construed narrowly to maximize the availability of government records, and the Supreme Court's construction of the exemptions, and FOIA in general, has become increasingly textualist. The exemptions are not mandatory bars to disclosure, and therefore an agency—unless otherwise prohibited by a more specific statute—may exercise its discretion to disclose exempted information. FOIA now explicitly requires agencies to apply a "foreseeable harm" standard in determining whether to withhold records the agency has the discretion to release because those records fall within an exception. Sometimes agencies will lose the power to withhold records due to public acknowledgement of the existence of the records or their content. This "public acknowledgement" doctrine is applied conservatively.

1. *The Exemptions*

Exemption 1 covers documents that are "specifically authorized under criteria established by an Executive Order to be kept secret in the interest of national defense or foreign policy and are in fact properly classified pursuant to such Executive Order."

The classification system is set out by the Information Security Oversight Office (ISOO) of the National Archives and Records Administration pursuant to Executive Order 13,526. The ISOO provisions, set forth in 32 C.F.R. parts 2001 and 2003, provide that information shall be considered for classification only where it concerns (1) military plans, weapons systems, or operations; (2) foreign government information; (3) intelligence activities (including special activities), intelligence sources or methods, or cryptology; (4) foreign relations or foreign activities of the United States, including confidential sources; (5) scientific, technological, or economic matters relating to the national security; (6) United States government programs for safeguarding nuclear materials or facilities; (7) vulnerabilities or capabilities of systems, installations, projects, or plans relating to the national security; or (8) the development, production, or use of weapons of mass destruction. The ISOO provisions prohibit classifying information to conceal violations of law, inefficiency, or administrative error; to prevent embarrassment to a person, organization, or the agency; to restrain competition; to prevent or delay the disclosure of information that does not warrant national security protection; or to thwart public access to basic scientific research not clearly related to national security. The designation of documents as "sensitive but unclassified" (SBU) or "controlled unclassified information" (CUI) or the like does not bring the document within the protection of Exemption 1, and thus such documents are subject to disclosure upon request unless covered by another exemption (e.g., the law enforcement exception) or an exclusion.

Courts afford substantial weight to an agency's affidavit concerning information classified under Exemption 1, sometimes describing the test they apply as the "logical and plausible" standard. An agency is entitled to summary judgment if its affidavits "describe the withheld information and the justification for withholding with reasonable specificity, demonstrating a logical connection between the information and the claimed exemption," and the affidavits "are not controverted by either contrary evidence in the record nor by evidence of bad faith." National security agencies may also refuse to confirm or deny the existence or nonexistence of requested information (known as a *Glomar* or "neither confirm nor deny" response) whenever the information's existence or nonexistence is also classified. Agencies have sometimes used a variation of the *Glomar* response, the "no number, no list" response, in which agencies acknowledge having records but do not enumerate them. Some courts have extended the availability of a neither-confirm-nor-deny response to protect information included within other exemptions.

Courts may conduct *in camera* review of information withheld under Exemption 1. Such review is not granted as a matter of course, and the courts consider several factors, including the likelihood that sensitive information might be inadvertently disclosed, in deciding whether to undertake such review. An agency may also make an *in camera* submission to support its classification decision, but the agency must make its reasons for doing so clear and "create as complete a public record as possible" for the party seeking disclosure. An *in camera* affidavit may be used where acknowledgement of certain records may pose a threat to national security, that is, where an agency uses a *Glomar* response to neither confirm nor deny the existence of a record. *In camera* affidavits may also be used where "the very association of the identities of the original classifying authorities" is "a classified fact."

Exemption 2 protects from disclosure information "related solely to the internal personnel rules and practices of an agency." *Milner v. Department of the Navy* provides the current standard for Exemption 2, which hews closely to the statutory text. The test for withholding a record under the exemption requires that the record contain *internal* agency information *solely* related to *"personnel" rules and practices.* To qualify as "internal," the record must be one the agency ordinarily keeps to itself for its own use.

The personnel rules and practices must be routine or trivial and thus not the sort of material in which the public could reasonably be expected to have an interest. The matters thus encompassed include matters relating to pay, pensions, vacations, hours of work, lunch hours, parking arrangements, and the like. Administrative markings on agency personnel files—such as file numbers, initials, signatures, routing marks, computer codes, access numbers, storage, location, retrieval markings, and the like—are also exempt. Some internal personnel records, for example, case summaries of honor and ethics code hearings concerning cadets at the nation's military academies, have been found to have substantial potential for public interest outside the government and thus do not qualify for Exemption 2.

The exemption does not protect documents concerning an agency's internal rules and practices providing direction for its personnel to follow in the discharge of their governmental functions. Caselaw recognizing a "high-2" exemption allowing agencies to withhold such materials that could facilitate circumvention of agency regulations or statutes, that is, material such as operating rules, guidelines, and manuals of procedure for government investigators or examiners, was repudiated by the U.S. Supreme Court in *Milner*, and is no longer good law. However, other exemptions, particularly the law enforcement exemption, may protect from disclosure some records that could facilitate circumvention of the law.

Exemption 3 protects information specifically exempted from disclosure by statute, provided that such statute (1) either (a) requires that the matters be withheld from the public in such a manner as to leave no discretion on the issue or (b) establishes particular criteria for withholding or refers to particular types of matters to be withheld, and (2) if enacted after March 17, 2009, the statute explicitly references Exemption 3. The courts have split on whether to afford deference to an agency's interpretation of a statute that purportedly authorizes nondisclosure. (With the Supreme Court's repudiation of *Chevron* deference in *Loper Bright Enterprises v. Raimondo*, this debate may shift.) The Department of Justice periodically publishes a list of statutes that courts have found to be Exemption 3 statutes.

Exemption 4 applies to "trade secrets" and to "commercial or financial information obtained from a person and privileged or confidential."

For purposes of Exemption 4, a trade secret includes any "unpatented, secret, commercially valuable plan, appliance, formula, or process, which is used for the making, preparing, compounding, treating, or processing of articles or materials which are trade commodities." A trade secret may also encompass a broader category of information, including any formula, pattern, device, or compilation of information used in a business and which gives the business a potential competitive advantage.

Virtually any information tied to commerce or business could qualify as "commercial or financial information" protected under Exemption 4, so long as the information has been generated by a person outside the government and is either privileged or confidential. Privileged information includes information that is covered by evidentiary privileges, such as the attorney-client privilege. Explicating the meaning of the term "confidential" has proven more complicated. The Supreme Court dramatically expanded the types of information that could be considered "confidential" in *Food Marketing Institute v. Argus Leader*. To be considered "confidential" under *Food Marketing*, business information must customarily be kept private (or at least closely held) by the entity that supplied the information to the government.

It is unclear whether, to fit within the definition of "confidentiality," the information must also be provided to the government under an assurance of confidentiality. The Supreme Court has not yet answered the question of whether this second element is mandatory, but the Department of Justice has instructed agencies to treat it as such.[1] An assurance of confidentiality need not be express but can be implied in some circumstances. In making such an assessment, an agency should consider its treatment of similar information as well as its broader treatment of information related to the program for which the information has been obtained. Context might negate an implicit assurance of confidentiality, such as when the agency's historical practice is to disclose such records or when the record reflects the government's own actions (such as its payments to a business entity for goods and service).

The *Food Marketing* definition of the term "confidential" displaces the long-standing *National Parks/Critical Mass* doctrine, which required inquiry into the particular consequences the release of commercial or financial information would have in terms of the potential competitive harm to the supplier of the information and the potential harm to the government's ability to obtain such information in the future. While such caselaw would appear to be rendered irrelevant by *Food Marketing*, agencies' judicially enforceable obligations to perform a "foreseeable harm" analysis to justify withholding records may require agencies to continue to release information unless they can show competitive harm to the provider of the information or harm to the agency's future ability to obtain the information.

Agencies must provide notice to submitters of confidential commercial information in advance of disclosure pursuant to executive order. (See Section III.)

Exemption 5 shields from mandatory disclosure "inter-agency or intra-agency memorandums or letters which would not be available by law to a party other than an agency in litigation with the agency." The exemption has three basic purposes—(1) to promote full, frank, and

1. In light of the new administration in 2025 with views significantly different from the former administration, it is possible that Department of Justice guidance may change.

candid policymaking debate within and among agencies; (2) to prevent premature disclosure of developing agency actions and policies; and (3) to enhance public knowledge of an agency's decision, by avoiding confusion between the actual basis for the agency's decisions and other bases the agency considered but ultimately did not choose to rely, or even opine, upon.

To qualify for protection, a document must satisfy two conditions: (1) its source must be a federal agency, and (2) it must fall within a privilege against discovery under judicial standards that would govern in litigation against the agency. With respect to the first condition, the source of the document may be an outside consultant hired by the agency who occupies the same position in the decisionmaking process as a government employee (i.e., the "consultant's corollary"). However, increasing skepticism has been expressed in some circuits regarding the validity of continued recognition of the consultant's corollary given its questionable basis in FOIA's text. Whatever protection the consultant's corollary accords does not extend to communications to or from an interested person or group seeking a government benefit at the expense of other applicants. This principle applies even if the group is a quasi-governmental body, such as an Indian tribe, to which the agency has trust obligations. It is not clear whether Exemption 5 can be invoked when the source of the document is a state government or a foreign government.

With respect to the second condition, the exemption includes all government litigation privileges, including the presidential communications privilege (i.e., "executive privilege"), the deliberative process privilege, and other traditional privileges such as the attorney-client and work product privileges. In applying the deliberative process privilege, a general distinction is made between deliberative and pre-decisional materials, which are afforded protection, and factual and post-decisional materials, which are not. Pre-decisional, deliberative documents lose their protection if adopted or incorporated by reference in the agency's final decision. In terms of assessing the finality of the agency's decision, what matters "is not whether a document is last in line, but whether it communicates a policy on which the agency has settled." A document may remain pre-decisional even if it is the last produced with respect to a matter, because some agency proposals "wither on the vine." Exemption 5 now explicitly provides that the deliberative process privilege protecting a record lapses after 25 years. Exemption 5 also offers some protection to confidential commercial information generated by the government in the process of awarding a contract (including Domestic Policy Directives and related documents generated in determining and implementing national monetary policy), factual statements made to government aircraft safety investigators under an assurance of confidentiality, and expert witness reports.

Exemption 6 covers "personnel and medical files and similar files the disclosure of which would constitute a clearly unwarranted invasion of personal privacy." Personnel files include files containing personal data such as date and place of birth, parents' names, residences, academic and professional evaluations, and the like. Medical files are those containing assessments or records of an individual's medical or psychological status. The category of "similar files" has "a broad, rather than a narrow, meaning" and includes any record that contains information regarding a natural person. The material need not be maintained in a file maintained on the individual by name or other identifier, distinguishing FOIA from the Privacy Act. Personal privacy encompasses only such interests of natural persons. Thus, artificial persons, such as corporations, are not considered to have "personal privacy" interests within the meaning of this exemption (though such entities' interests in confidentiality are protected by Exemption 4). That said, a person engaging in a business, by way of a sole proprietorship or closely held corporation, can have a "personal privacy" interest in certain matters related to that business.

The concept of privacy encompasses individuals' interest in control of information concerning themselves reflected in both the common law and the nation's cultural traditions, and thus extends beyond the common law definition of privacy interests. The concept of privacy includes both the prosaic and the intimate and potentially embarrassing, as well as information that might result in inconvenience or reprisals. Thus, a cognizable privacy invasion exists if disclosure would invite unwarranted intrusion into an individual's privacy, even if the disclosure, by itself, would not cause embarrassment. Exemption 6 applies only where the invasion of personal privacy is real, as opposed to speculative. Either the author of a document or its subject may assert their own privacy interest in preventing disclosure of the document. Mailing lists and other compilations of names are generally covered by Exemption 6.

While public availability of information will ordinarily negate a claim of privacy, a privacy interest may sometimes exist even if the information has, at some point, been made public, such as when the information remains "practically obscure." This concept has been applied to "rap sheets" compiled by federal law enforcement agencies.

The determination of whether a disclosure constitutes a "clearly unwarranted" invasion of privacy requires balancing the privacy interest against the public interest in disclosure, with a tilt in favor of disclosure. So far, the Supreme Court has recognized only one cognizable "public interest" in disclosure—the disclosure's potential contribution to the public's understanding of *government* operations or activities. The Supreme Court has left open the question of whether such a public interest might encompass the potential "derivative uses" of information that would facilitate private monitoring of government activity. To the extent that the requested information reveals that a senior government official engaged in wrongdoing or misconduct, disclosure is likely in order, because the public is entitled to learn about infractions committed by senior officials.

If information is covered by both Exemption 6 and the Privacy Act, 5 U.S.C. § 552a, because the Privacy Act forbids agency disclosure of an individual's records to third parties, the information may not be disclosed to a third party even if a public interest in disclosure can be shown. However, FOIA exemptions cannot be used to withhold a "first-party" request for information pursuant to the Privacy Act. Because individuals who are not citizens or lawful permanent residents cannot use the Privacy Act, many immigration lawyers use FOIA to obtain their client's immigration records in order to facilitate seeking relief on the client's behalf.

Exemption 7 protects "records or information compiled for law enforcement purposes," but only to the extent that their disclosure would have one of six specific harms. Protection is not limited to "investigatory files," the term originally used in FOIA, but broadly covers any "records or information," including, for example, law enforcement manuals. The term "compiled" encompasses more than records and information originally compiled and still maintained for law enforcement purposes. It includes records and information originally compiled for such purposes but subsequently reproduced or summarized in a new document for a non-law-enforcement purpose. It includes, as well, materials initially obtained or generated for non-law-enforcement purposes and subsequently compiled for a law enforcement purpose.

"Law enforcement purposes" encompasses criminal prosecutions, civil enforcement, and administrative enforcement efforts. The term also encompasses proactive steps designed to prevent criminal activity and to maintain national and homeland security. While "law enforcement" does not include general agency monitoring of its employees to ensure compliance with applicable requirements, it can include an agency's investigation of an employee's illegal conduct.

Agencies must establish a nexus between the information they seek to withhold and their law enforcement functions. The level of scrutiny applied to this nexus requirement varies depending on the type of agency involved; courts distinguish between agencies principally engaged in criminal law enforcement and multipurpose agencies pursuing dual law enforcement and administrative functions. For law enforcement agencies, the circuit courts have primarily adopted one of two deferential standards—the "rational nexus test" or the *per se* rule. Under the rational nexus approach, the agency must specify the nexus between the requested information and its law enforcement duties, and the agency's explanation of the nexus will be reviewed for rationality. Under the *per se* approach, courts presume a sufficient nexus. For multifunction agencies, the nexus test is applied with greater exactitude.

Exemption 7(A) protects law enforcement records and information, the disclosure of which "could reasonably be expected to interfere with enforcement proceedings." For records to qualify under Exemption 7(A), the government must show that (1) an enforcement proceeding is pending or prospective, and (2) the requested record's release could reasonably be expected to cause some articulable harm to that proceeding. Such harms include assisting possible witness intimidation, deterring future witnesses from providing information or testifying, and allowing potential defendants to construct defenses that permit violations to go unchecked. Though Exemption 7(A) requires the existence of a pending or prospective law enforcement action, the exemption may properly be invoked where one particular case has been closed but further enforcement action may be taken.

Exemption 7(B) applies where disclosure of law enforcement records or information "would deprive a person of a right to fair trial or an impartial adjudication."

To justify nondisclosure, the government must show "(1) that a trial or adjudication is pending or truly imminent and (2) that it is more probable than not that disclosure of the material sought would seriously interfere with the fairness of those proceedings." Serious interference with the fairness of proceedings includes publicity of such a nature and degree as to compromise judicial fairness, and disclosures of information not available under discovery rules that would confer an unfair advantage upon a party to the proceeding. However, the exemption does not protect documents merely because a civil proceeding between private parties is pending and the court has not ordered the documents to be turned over in discovery.

Exemption 7(C) protects law enforcement records and information, the disclosure of which could reasonably be expected to constitute an unwarranted invasion of privacy. This language differs from that in Exemption 6, regarding personnel and medical files, *inter alia*, which permits withholding if a record's release would constitute a *"clearly unwarranted"* invasion of privacy. As a consequence, protection of privacy is more robust under Exemption 7(C) for law enforcement records. Nevertheless, like Exemption 6, Exemption 7(C) requires a balancing of the public interest in disclosure against the invasion of personal privacy. Exemption 7(C) may be used to protect the identities of persons connected to law enforcement activities, including subjects of investigations, informants who do not qualify for protection under Exemption 7(D), FBI agents, other officers involved in investigations, and individuals otherwise connected to criminal investigations.

For purposes of Exemption 7(C), a third party's request for law enforcement records or information about a private citizen can reasonably be expected to invade that citizen's privacy. Such an invasion of privacy is "unwarranted" if the request seeks no "official information" about a government agency but merely records that the government happens to be storing.

The relevant privacy interest is not limited to information about oneself; release of information about a person may constitute an unwarranted invasion of the privacy of that person's family members. For example, family members may assert a privacy interest in the crime scene photographs of a deceased family member. As with Exemption 6, the "personal privacy" interests protected by Exemption 7(C) are those of natural persons; thus, the exemption may not be invoked to protect the "privacy" of a corporation.

As already noted, a privacy interest may be overcome by showing a sufficiently strong interest in public disclosure. Sometimes, the asserted public interest in disclosure is revelation of government officials' negligent or otherwise improper performance of their duties. In such circumstances, however, the requester must establish more than a bare suspicion of such negligence or misconduct. Rather, the requester must produce evidence that would warrant a belief by a reasonable person that the alleged government impropriety might have occurred.

Exemption 7(D) protects law enforcement records and information that could reasonably be expected to identify a confidential source, including a state, local, or foreign agency or authority or any private institution that has furnished information on a confidential basis. Exemption 7(D) also covers the information furnished by a confidential source or information compiled either by a criminal law enforcement authority in the course of a criminal investigation or by an agency conducting a lawful national security intelligence investigation.

Exemption 7(D) extends to a broad group of information purveyors the most comprehensive protection for law enforcement information that FOIA affords. Information provided by a source is considered confidential if the source reasonably believed that the information would remain confidential, even if the information is contained in a document that the agency does not usually treat as such. The identity of a source is protected whenever the source has provided information under express assurance of confidentiality or under circumstances from which such an assurance could reasonably be inferred.

Exemption 7(D) is unlimited in duration; its protections remain undiminished despite the conclusion of the investigation, the end of the prosecution, or even the source's death. Where an informant has testified in open court, the government may still invoke the exemption to protect information not disclosed during that testimony.

Exemption 7(E) covers law enforcement records and information that would disclose techniques and procedures for law enforcement investigations or prosecutions, or would disclose guidelines for law enforcement investigations or prosecutions if such disclosure could reasonably be expected to allow violators of the law to circumvent law enforcement and evade detection. There is some confusion regarding whether the clause regarding risk of circumvention and evasion refers to "techniques and procedures" as well as "guidelines for law enforcement investigations and prosecutions."

The exemption protects from disclosure techniques and procedures not well known to the public and, in addition, covers even commonly known procedures and techniques where the relevant disclosure might diminish their effectiveness.

Exemption 7(F) protects law enforcement records and information, the disclosure of which could reasonably be expected to endanger the life or physical safety of any individual. Unlike Exemption 7(C), Exemption 7(F) contains no balancing requirement. It is not clear whether the government need show any more than potential "diffuse harms to unknown and unspecified individuals" or must identify at least one endangered individual or discrete population.

Exemption 8 applies to matters "contained in or related to examination, operating, or condition reports prepared by, on behalf of, or for the use of an agency responsible for the regulation or supervision of financial institutions." The term "financial institutions" is not limited to depository institutions, but can include institutions that provide credit services, the Financial Institutions Regulatory Authority (FINRA), debt collectors, investor advisor companies, securities brokers and dealers, and self-regulatory organizations. All records that concern a covered entity's financial condition and operations that are in the possession and control of a federal agency tasked with the regulation or supervision of financial institutions are exempt from disclosure. Exemption 8 was intended by Congress, and has been interpreted by the courts, to be very broadly construed to both ensure the security of financial institutions and safeguard the relationship between financial institutions and their supervising agencies. Thus, in the context of Exemption 8, the "foreseeable harm" standard should be applied with "extreme care" to avoid diminishing the protection traditionally afforded by the courts under the exemption. By statute, Exemption 8's applicability is more limited with respect to some aspects of the Federal Deposit Insurance Corporation's (FDIC) reports.

Exemption 9 applies to "geological and geophysical information and data, including maps, concerning wells." Wells encompassed by Exemption 9 include not just wells related to the development of oil and natural gas but also wells used in exploiting underground water sources.

2. *The Foreseeable Harm Standard*

Even when an agency concludes that a record falls within one of FOIA's exemptions, it must nevertheless make the information available unless either (1) the agency "reasonably foresees that disclosure would harm an interest protected by" the exemption or (2) the disclosure is prohibited by law. As to the first, the "foreseeable harm standard," mere "speculative or abstract fears" are insufficient to satisfy the standard. The standard is not meant to displace equivalent or more demanding foreseeable harm standards set forth in the text of specific exemptions, including several in the law enforcement exemption. For example, Exemptions 7(B) and 7(D), respectively, prohibit release of law enforcement records or information "that would deprive a person of a right to a fair trial or an impartial adjudication" or "could reasonably be expected to disclose the identity of a confidential source." Similarly, Exemption 7(E) prohibits disclosure of law enforcement guidelines for investigations or prosecutions "if such disclosure could reasonably be expected to risk circumvention of the law."

The foreseeable harm standard does not require release of records whose disclosure is otherwise prohibited. For example, because disclosure of classified information is a criminal offense, an agency need not assess whether disclosure of properly classified information could reasonably be expected to harm the national security interests protected by Exemption 1. And many documents covered by the privacy exemptions, Exemptions 6 and 7(C), will not be subject to a foreseeable harm analysis to the extent that the Privacy Act precludes their disclosure. Documents falling within Exemption 4 may not be subject to the "foreseeable harm" standard to the extent that the Trade Secrets Act prohibits their release. Reflecting a similar rationale, section 555(a)(8)(B) makes clear that the foreseeable harm assessment does not apply to records withheld under Exemption 3, which incorporates by reference statutes that generally leave agencies no room for discretion with regard to disclosing certain records or information.

The obligation to consider segregations and partial release of a record is applicable to records withheld because harm is reasonably foreseeable or disclosure of some portion of the record is prohibited by law.

The agency's application of, or failure to apply, the foreseeable harm standard is subject to judicial review. The foreseeable harm standard "impose[s] an independent and meaningful burden on agencies." Thus, the inquiries into whether a record fits within an exemption and whether its release will cause foreseeable harm are "distinct, consecutive inquiries." Agency affidavits must provide "a focused and concrete" analysis "of why disclosure of the particular type of material at issue will, in the specific context of the agency action at issue, actually impede" the interests protected by the FOIA exemption invoked. "Boilerplate and generic assertions," or "perfunctory, sweeping, and undifferentiated" justifications encompassing all documents falling with an exemption will ordinarily be insufficient.

3. *The Public Acknowledgement Doctrine*

An agency cannot invoke exemptions to withhold information it has "officially acknowledged." Generally, this principle also extends to information that is otherwise legitimately in the public domain. However, in a related context, involving invocation of the state secrets privilege, the Supreme Court has said "[i]n certain circumstances, the Government may assert the state secrets privilege to bar the confirmation or denial of information that has entered the public domain through unofficial sources."

The agency's invocation of an exemption is barred under the "official acknowledgement" doctrine only when the information requested (1) is as specific as the information previously released, (2) matches the information previously disclosed, and (3) has already been made public through an official and documented disclosure. Official acknowledgement is agency specific; one agency's release of information does not preclude another from invoking an exemption for its records containing such information. Application of the "official acknowledgement" doctrine may, to some extent, be dependent upon the exemption invoked. For example, the doctrine is applied quite strictly with respect to classified materials protected under Exemption 1. Where individual privacy interests are at stake, only the individual whose informational privacy interests are protected can effect a waiver. The FOIA plaintiff bears the burden of production regarding official acknowledgement.

The "official acknowledgement" analysis differs somewhat when a FOIA plaintiff seeks to overcome an agency's *Glomar* (i.e., "neither confirm nor deny") response, focusing on whether the agency has already disclosed the fact of the existence of responsive records. "Official acknowledgement" is sufficient to overcome a *Glomar* response only if the official acknowledgements leave no doubt that the agency possesses responsive records.

D. Exclusions

Records covered by an exclusion from FOIA are treated "as not subject to the requirements of" the act. When documents requested fall within one of the exclusions, the agency will respond by stating that no responsive records exist. FOIA sets forth three exclusions. Exclusion (c)(1) applies to Exemption 7(A) materials where there is a criminal investigation and authorities have reason to believe that (1) the subject of the investigation is unaware that it is ongoing and (2) disclosure of the records could reasonably be expected to interfere with enforcement efforts. Exclusion (c)(2) applies to requests for information involving the threatened identification of confidential informants in criminal proceedings. Exclusion (c)(3) applies to classified records kept by the FBI relating to foreign intelligence, counterintelligence, and international terrorism.

II. JUDICIAL REVIEW

A. Jurisdiction

Under FOIA, federal jurisdiction is dependent upon a showing that an agency has (1) "improperly," (2) "withheld," (3) "agency records." Federal district courts have exclusive jurisdiction to enjoin an agency from withholding agency records and order production of any records improperly withheld. District courts also have jurisdiction to determine whether an agency has charged excessive fees for responding to a FOIA request and whether the agency has improperly denied a fee waiver request. Courts have jurisdiction to review an agency's failure to publish information required by section 552(a)(1) and its refusal to make information available in its electronic reading room under section 552(a)(2). There is a circuit split regarding when a court can order an agency that violates section 552(a)(2) to post records mandated to be made available to the public or can merely order the agency to make such records available to the particular FOIA requester.

B. Pattern or Practice Claims

Typically, FOIA cases are brought to obtain documents the agency has withheld in response to a particular FOIA request. At least two courts of appeals, the D.C. Circuit and the Ninth, as well as several district courts in other circuits, have recognized broader pattern or practice claims, in which the party seeks injunctive relief against an agency pattern of behavior or practice that violates FOIA. Recognition of such cases is not without dispute, and the Supreme Court has yet to resolve the issue. In such pattern and practice cases, plaintiff must still show that the agency has (1) "improperly," (2) "withheld," (3) "agency records." In such cases, plaintiffs "must show that they are suffering an ongoing injury or face an immediate threat of future injury." Generally speaking, this requirement can be established by showing the plaintiff has several pending FOIA requests that will be implicated by the alleged pattern or practice. Most cases to date that address pattern or practice claims appear to have involved issues regarding delay in providing records or other procedural deficiencies, rather than the scope of exemptions.

C. Exhaustion of Administrative Remedies

FOIA requesters must exhaust administrative remedies before filing suit. Administrative remedies "shall be deemed" exhausted if the agency fails to comply with the applicable time limit provisions. If the agency responds to an initial request after the 20 working days permitted for a response to the request, but prior to the filing of a lawsuit, the requester is obligated to pursue an administrative appeal prior to initiating litigation.

Even if an agency fails to meet the time limits and the requester brings suit, courts may stay the litigation, retain jurisdiction, and allow the agency additional time to process the request if the agency can show that "exceptional circumstances exist and the agency is exercising due diligence in responding to the request." Exceptional circumstances exist only where the agency "is deluged with a volume of requests for information vastly in excess of that anticipated by Congress" and "the existing resources are inadequate to deal with the volume of such requests within the time limits" of the act. Such stays are referred to as "Open America" stays.

D. Statute of Limitations

The general federal statute of limitations of six years applies to FOIA suits and begins to run once the requester has, or is deemed to have, exhausted his administrative remedies. However, the limitation does not restrict a requester from making a subsequent request for the same documents and litigating the withholding of documents in connection with the subsequent request.

E. Venue

Venue for a FOIA action is in the federal district in which an individual plaintiff resides, or a business or organizational plaintiff has its principal place of business, or the district in which the agency records are situated, or in the District of Columbia.

F. Burden of Proof

The agency always has the burden of proving (1) that the records in question or any parts withheld are exempt from disclosure, and (2) that each document requested either has been produced, is unidentifiable, or is wholly exempt from disclosure.

As a general rule, the agency must assert all exemptions at the same time, in the original district court proceedings. However, courts have allowed assertion of additional exemptions when the failure to assert them initially resulted from a mistake and the failure to allow assertion of the exemption would put the safety or privacy of a third party at risk. The agency may rely in the district court on an exemption it did not raise administratively.

G. *De Novo* Review

Agency decisions to withhold information are reviewed *de novo* by the courts. The adequacy of searches is also reviewed *de novo*. Such *de novo* review is not to be confused with the Administrative Procedure Act's provision regarding judicial review of facts subject to "trial de novo," namely 5 U.S.C. § 706(2)(F). The contemporaneous administrative record in FOIA cases is often sparse and frequently supplemented by affidavits or declarations (collectively "affidavits") submitted by government records custodians or government officials after the litigation has commenced (a practice that is rare in most judicial review of agency decisions). Moreover, the agency affidavits generally enjoy a presumption of "good faith," requiring requesters to rebut assertions made in the affidavits. Thus, FOIA cases are ordinarily resolved on summary judgment based on facts set forth in the government affidavits as well as the almost always quite limited "administrative record." If the government affidavits and the administrative record are inadequate, the court will most likely either order supplementation of the affidavits by the agency or conduct an *in camera* review of some of the documents, rather than conducting trial-type proceedings.

There has been some inconsistency regarding the standard of review applied by courts of appeals reviewing district court decisions. The weight of contemporary authority appears to be that such review is conducted *de novo*. However, there is some older authority employing a "clear error" standard wherein once the court decides that the government affidavits provide a sufficient ground for decision, the district court's decision is reviewed on a "clear error" standard.

H. *Vaughn* Index

Courts usually require agencies in FOIA litigation to provide the requester with a detailed explanation of the agency's refusal to disclose requested documents. This "*Vaughn* index" must include (1) an itemization and description of the records withheld, (2) a detailed justification for the claim of exemption, and (3) an index cross-referencing the justification with the record or portion thereof to which it applies. There is "no fixed rule" establishing what such an affidavit must look like; the index's functional attributes, not its form, are critical. Courts have discretion to refuse a requester's motion seeking a *Vaughn* index or to require the submission of the index for *in camera* review.

An agency may organize its *Vaughn* index on a "category-of-document by category-of-document basis, so long as the agency's definitions of relevant categories are sufficiently distinct to allow a court to determine whether specific claimed exemptions are properly applied." The "range of circumstances included in the category must 'characteristically support' an inference that the statutory requirements for exemption are satisfied."

I. *In Camera* Inspection

Courts have broad discretionary power to conduct an *in camera* review of disputed information. See, for example, Section I.C.1.

J. Discovery

Discovery is available in FOIA cases, but usually courts severely restrict its scope. Discovery is appropriate to determine the scope of the agency's search for responsive records or to investigate factual questions concerning whether the agency's exemption claim is well founded. Discovery may not be had where the plaintiff is seeking to obtain information contained in the withheld records or to question investigatory activities undertaken by the agency.

K. Attorneys' Fees and Costs

A court may assess against the United States reasonable attorney's fees and other litigation costs reasonably incurred in any FOIA case in which the complainant substantially prevails. The agency must pay such an award directly out of its own budget. In awarding fees and costs, courts generally consider four criteria: (1) the public benefit, if any, from the case; (2) the commercial benefit to the plaintiff; (3) the nature of the plaintiff's interest in the records sought; and (4) the reasonableness of the government's legal position in withholding the records.

For a plaintiff to be considered to have "substantially prevail[ed]," the plaintiff must have "obtained relief." Such relief need not have been obtained through a judicial order or consent decree; a voluntary or unilateral change in the agency's position suffices. The plaintiff need not have won the release of all requested records, but the litigation must have had a substantially causative effect on the release of information by the agency. Even where no records are released, however, the requester may be deemed to have "substantially prevailed" if the suit compels an agency to comply with the law.

L. Sanctions

Sanctions may be imposed against employees of an agency for failing to comply with FOIA. A proceeding for sanctions may be initiated by the United States Office of Special Counsel when (1) a court orders production of an agency record improperly withheld; (2) the court assesses reasonable attorney's fees and other litigation costs against the government; and (3) the court issues a written finding that the circumstances surrounding the withholding suggest that agency personnel acted arbitrarily and capriciously.

III. SUITS TO ENJOIN DISCLOSURE (REVERSE-FOIA CASES)

A person who has submitted information to the government has a legally cognizable interest in that information and may seek judicial review under the APA of an agency's decision to grant a FOIA request for the information or otherwise release that information. While FOIA itself places no constraints on release of information held by government agencies, other laws may constrain agency discretion to make disclosures under FOIA. The party seeking to prevent the disclosure of information bears the burden of justifying nondisclosure. Executive Order 12,600 requires agencies to issue regulations allowing submitters of information to the government to designate the information as potentially causing competitive harm if released. The regulations must also provide for notice to submitters that the agency has determined it may be required to release such records, and to "give careful consideration to" submitters' objections to the release. If the agency determines not to release the information, and the requester files suit to compel disclosure, the submitter should also be notified of such suit.

IV. FEDERAL ADVISORY COMMITTEE ACT

The Federal Advisory Committee Act (FACA), 5 U.S.C. §§ 1001–1014, in general, applies to any committee not wholly composed of federal employees established by statute, or established or utilized by the executive branch, for the purpose of providing advice to the President or to one or more agencies or officers of the federal government. The act's requirements do not apply to subcommittees as long as they do not function as, or make decisions that bind, the full committee.

An advisory committee is "established" for purposes of FACA only if the government itself has "organized" or "formed" the committee. Whether a committee is "utilized" within the meaning of the FACA depends on three factors: (1) whether the committee was formed at the federal government's prompting, (2) whether the government exercised control over the committee's operations or affairs, and (3) whether the committee received federal funding.

An advisory committee is subject to FACA only where it renders advice to the President, the Congress, or an executive branch agency, including any independent regulatory agency.

FACA requires covered committees to be fairly balanced in terms of the points of view represented and the functions to be performed, although courts have not been demanding in their interpretation of this provision. Before an advisory committee meets or takes action, a charter for it must be filed with (1), in the case of presidential advisory committees, the administrator of the General Services Administration, or (2) the agency head to whom the advisory committee reports and the standing committees of the Senate and the House of Representatives having legislative jurisdiction over the agency. The charter must set forth the committee's objectives and scope, the time period necessary for it to carry out its functions, the agency responsible for providing the committee support, and the duties for which the committee is responsible.

The public must be given timely notice of committee meetings (at least 15 days in advance) through publication of the committee's agenda in the *Federal Register*. Advisory committee meetings must be open to the public, unless the President or the head of the agency to which the advisory committee reports determines that the meeting may be closed in accordance with the exemptions listed in the Government in the Sunshine Act. Individuals may "attend, appear before, or file statements" with the committee, subject to reasonable regulations. Records, reports, transcripts, minutes, agendas, working papers, drafts, or other documents made available to or prepared by an advisory committee shall be made available to the public, except to the extent that the material is protected from disclosure under one or more applicable FOIA exemptions.

Each agency is responsible for providing support services to its advisory committees, and each advisory committee meeting must be chaired or attended by a designated government officer. Each committee has a two-year life span, unless a different period is specified by statute or the committee's creating authority takes action to renew its existence. The provisions of FACA may be enforced by a private action under the APA against the agency to which the committee reports, although courts are divided as to the scope of relief available.

FACA also requires that agencies make available to any person, at actual cost of duplication, copies of transcripts of agency proceedings or advisory committee meetings.

V. GOVERNMENT IN THE SUNSHINE ACT

The Government in the Sunshine Act, codified primarily at 5 U.S.C. § 552b, applies to any agency subject to FOIA and headed by a collegial body of two or more individual members, a majority of whom are appointed by the President with the advice and consent of the Senate, and to any subdivision of such an agency authorized to act on its behalf.

An agency subject to the Sunshine Act must give reasonable notice of its meetings and make every portion of its meetings open to public observation, unless the agency has properly decided to close the meeting, or a portion thereof, pursuant to one of the act's ten exemptions. The act does not give the public a right to participate at meetings. Moreover, the act does not preclude collegial bodies from deciding matters without holding meetings, such as by members placing notations indicating concurrence or dissent on a packet of material laying out the issues and proposed resolution.

The act's exemptions permitting closure of meetings generally mirror those in FOIA, with two notable exceptions: internal privileged communications that would not prematurely disclose proposed agency actions (FOIA Exemption 5) are not included, while discussions of most agency adjudicatory matters are. An agency may not close any portion of a meeting without a majority of the members voting to close that portion of the meeting. The agency has the burden of proving that the decision to close a meeting was lawful.

For purposes of the act, the term "meeting" means the deliberations of at least the number of individuals required to take action on behalf of the agency where such deliberations determine or result in the joint conduct or disposition of official agency business, except that discussions of administrative matters such as scheduling a future meeting do not constitute meetings. Thus, a gathering of a subset of board members that does not constitute a quorum of the board is not a covered meeting. In addition, a meeting even of a quorum is not a "meeting" subject to the open meeting requirement if it is not "sufficiently focused on discrete proposals or issues as to cause or to be likely to cause the individual participating members to form reasonably firm positions regarding matters pending or likely to arise before the agency." Meetings include not only sessions in which members of the body are physically present in the same location but also sessions in which members interact contemporaneously by telephone or other technological means. It is not clear whether the act covers non-contemporaneous digital or electronic interactions between members, such as by way of email.

The act provides district courts with subject matter jurisdiction to enforce the requirements of the act relating to open meetings and records by declaratory judgment, injunctive relief, or other appropriate relief. Invalidation of the agency action is not a proper remedy under the act, but requiring a meeting to be open or records to be disclosed is. A prevailing party is entitled to reasonable attorney's fees and other litigation costs.

PART SIX

GOVERNMENT MANAGEMENT OF THE ADMINISTRATIVE PROCESS

PART SIX
GOVERNMENT MANAGEMENT OF THE ADMINISTRATIVE PROCESS

I. SCOPE

Part Six concerns procedures relating to the management of administrative functions across federal agencies. These involve statutes, constitutional requirements, and executive orders.

II. CONGRESSIONAL MANAGEMENT OF AGENCY ACTION

The Constitution prohibits members or houses of Congress, or Congress itself, from being, appointing, or removing officers of the United States, or from vetoing an agency action other than through the enactment of legislation. Therefore, Congress has no power of direct supervision or management over agencies even though its power to define and limit an agency's authority is virtually plenary within the bounds of the Constitution.

Nevertheless, Congress has the recognized constitutional authority to oversee agency action for a number of purposes, especially for determining whether new legislation is necessary or appropriate. Congress's ultimate control over the agency's budget and its organic statute means that congressional views will have influence with the agency. Also, inherent in the legislative power is a power of inquiry, including the power to subpoena witnesses and documents (subject to applicable privileges, including an executive privilege of uncertain scope). This power of inquiry can be enforced against reluctant persons through the contempt power. However, when a federal officer refuses to appear or to produce documents pursuant to the direction of the attorney general, the Justice Department will not enforce the contempt citation in court.

Congressional investigation and public hearings can lead to public scrutiny and political pressure on the agency.

Attempts by members or committees of Congress to influence the outcome of an agency proceeding are subject to the APA's constraints on ex parte communications and other restrictions that apply to such attempts by private persons. Beyond those requirements, however, congressional attempts to influence agency proceedings are largely unregulated. Use of the congressional hearing power to try to influence the outcome of a pending formal adjudication has been held a violation of due process, although hearings to explore policy issues that might be involved in an adjudication can be permissible and appropriate if properly managed. Outside the context of formal or other on-the-record proceedings, a court is not likely to set aside an agency decision because of alleged congressional influence, unless the evidence shows that the pressure brought to bear caused the agency action to be affected by factors that are not relevant under the governing statute.

Under the Congressional Review Act, 5 U.S.C. §§ 801–808, a rule cannot take effect or continue in effect if Congress passes and the President signs a joint resolution disapproving a rule. Further, the agency is prohibited from issuing the same or a substantially similar rule absent future congressional authorization. The act exempts rules relating to agency management or personnel or agency organization, procedure, or practice, as well as rules of particular applicability. Non-legislative rules, such as interpretive rules and general statements of policy, however, are rules subject to the act. Before a rule can take effect, the promulgating agency must submit a copy of the rule and a concise general statement relating thereto to both houses of Congress and the comptroller general. A joint resolution of disapproval must be introduced within 60 legislative days of such submission and is considered according to expedited procedures set out in the act. A *major* rule *cannot* take effect for 60 calendar days after it has been submitted to Congress, a delay designed to ensure Congress has time to disapprove the rule. Moreover, if a rule is submitted near the end of a session of Congress, an additional period of time is afforded to allow the new session of Congress to consider the rule. This is called the "lookback provision."

Major rules include any rule (other than one promulgated under the Telecommunications Act of 1996 and its amendments) that the administrator of the Office of Management and Budget's Office of Information and Regulatory Affairs (OIRA) finds will result in an annual effect on the economy of $100 million or more; a major increase in costs or prices; or significant adverse effects on competition, employment, investment, productivity, or the ability of U.S.–based enterprises to compete with foreign enterprises.

The Congressional Review Act contains a provision precluding judicial review of any determination, finding, action, or omission under the act. As a result, the enforcement of the act is through the political process.

III. PRESIDENTIAL MANAGEMENT OF AGENCY ACTION

A. President's Constitutional Authority

Two provisions of Article II of the Constitution are conceived to be the primary sources of the President's authority to manage agency action. The first, known as the Vesting Clause, states that the "executive power" shall be vested in the President. U.S. Const., art. II, § 1, cl. 1. The second, known as the Take Care Clause, states that the President "shall take care that the laws be faithfully executed." U.S. Const., art. II, § 3. In addition, the President may "require the opinion, in writing, of the principal officer in each of the executive departments, upon any subject relating to the duties of their respective offices." U.S. Const., art. II, § 2, cl. 1. These provisions furnish authority to the President to supervise, consult with, and obtain information from executive officers in the performance of their statutory duties. For these purposes, an executive department includes cabinet departments, independent executive agencies, and independent regulatory commissions.

However, most statutes place rulemaking and adjudicatory authority in the agency head or the agency itself, not in the President. The extent to which the President can order agency officials to take actions within the officials' delegated authority is uncertain, but the President may remove agency heads for failure to follow his requests. However, under existing law, he cannot remove members of independent regulatory commissions except for cause.[1]

In practice, the President's exercise of his supervisory power has largely correlated with his ability on the one hand to appoint, with the advice and consent of the Senate, principal officers, U.S. Const., art. II, § 2, cl. 2, and on the other hand to remove agency officials who ignore his direction. While the Constitution may be read to preclude any statutory limitation on the President's appointment power, it is not uncommon for a statute creating an agency to place some limits on whom the President may appoint to head the agency. No cases have addressed the constitutionality of such limits, but Presidents since Ronald Reagan have issued signing statements to the effect that some such limitations are an unconstitutional restriction on the President's appointment powers.

The Constitution, other than in the impeachment clause, does not address who may remove executive officers or on what basis, but impeachment is by no means the only permissible route to removal of executive officers. Where statutes do not address removal of particular officers, it is presumed that the President may remove them at will, even if the office is for a term of years, except perhaps when their sole function is the adjudication of administrative cases.[2] Thus, under these circumstances, the President may remove an official simply for failure to follow supervision.

A number of statutes provide that an officer may be removed only for cause. Exactly what kind of conduct can constitute "cause" is unclear, but in practice removals on this basis are rare, and the Court has never directly addressed the issue. However, in a case involving the ability of Congress to remove the comptroller general for "inefficiency,"

---

1. The for-cause removal protection for members of independent regulatory commissions is currently being litigated in lower courts and will ultimately be decided by the Supreme Court.

2. Whether purely adjudicatory bodies are exempt from the President's otherwise constitutional power to remove officers appointed by the President is currently in litigation.

"neglect of duty," and "malfeasance," it characterized these terms as very broad and said they could be interpreted to include "any number of actual or perceived transgressions of the legislative will."

With respect to principal officers, under existing caselaw only members of multimember agencies may be protected from removal except for cause. Thus, single heads of agencies must be removable at will by the President. Inferior officers, however, may be provided with for cause removal protection, unless their superiors also have for cause removal protection. The status of administrative law judges (ALJs) is unclear, because they have "for-cause" removal protection but can only be removed upon a finding of the Merit Systems Protection Board, whose members also can only be removed for cause, and some of whom are employed by agencies whose members can only be removed for cause. Because ALJs only adjudicate cases, as opposed to making policy or engaging in enforcement activities, they may be an exception to the general rule against double for-cause removal protection.[3]

B. Regulatory Review

Although the specifics have varied with each administration, all Presidents since Richard Nixon have issued executive orders that require executive agencies, but not independent regulatory commissions, to perform certain analyses and submit certain proposed and final rules to an office in the Executive Office of the President for its review before publication. President Trump has eliminated the exception for independent regulatory commissions. Since President Reagan's E.O. 12,291 (1981), responsibility for such review has been lodged with OIRA, and the rules subject to review made more extensive. The procedural requirements of such review are set out above in Part Two, Section IV.

The relevant executive orders have also included provisions concerning regulatory planning, including the semiannual publication of an agenda describing all regulations each agency has under

3. Cases involving ALJ protections from removal are currently in litigation.

development or review. Under the current governing order, President Clinton's E.O. 12,866, as amended, agencies must prepare an annual Regulatory Plan (Plan), submitted to OIRA and included in the Unified Agenda of Federal Regulatory and Deregulatory Actions (Agenda). The Agenda describes and justifies the most important significant regulatory actions that the agency reasonably expects to issue in proposed or final form in that fiscal year or thereafter. E.O. 12,866 extended these planning requirements to independent regulatory commissions as well as executive agencies. President Trump's E.O. 14,192 stipulates that no regulation may be added to or removed from the Unified Regulatory Agenda without the approval of the director and that unless a regulation is included in the most recent version or update of the published Unified Agenda, it may not be issued without the written approval of the OMB director. The Agenda is published each fall and spring on OMB's website, reginfo.gov, and the Plan, which is prepared for the fall Agenda, is also published in the *Federal Register*.

Current executive orders, which are by definition subject to rescission or revision by successor administrations, also require or encourage the pursuit of specific substantive policies by requiring agencies to (1) prepare a cost-benefit analysis for economically significant regulatory actions; (2) pursue the most cost-effective regulatory alternative as a regulatory principle; (3) consider the impacts of proposed regulations on certain specified interests, such as federalism, the environmental health and safety of children, Indian tribal governments, takings of private property, and energy supply distribution and use; and (4) undertake periodic review of existing rules. President Trump has required in particular that, subject to exemptions and waivers granted by OMB, whenever an agency proposes or otherwise promulgates a new significant regulation, it shall identify at least ten existing regulations to be repealed. The new regulation's costs must be offset by the elimination of existing costs associated with at least ten prior regulations. Further, OMB must provide each agency with a total amount of incremental costs (akin to a "regulatory budget") that it will be allowed in issuing new regulations and repealing regulations for the next fiscal year.

Most executive orders governing agency rulemaking provide, as they must under the Constitution, that their provisions apply only "to the extent permitted by law." A violation of their requirements does not affect the validity of the rule or provide a basis for judicial review. Enforcement of the provisions of the oversight orders is left to the political process.

IV. STATUTORY REQUIREMENTS

A. Paperwork Reduction Act

The Paperwork Reduction Act of 1980, which covers essentially all executive branch agencies (including independent regulatory commissions and the Executive Office of the President) except the Federal Election Commission, applies to agency "collection of information." This term includes an agency's (1) collecting facts or information from ten or more persons, (2) requiring ten or more persons to disclose facts or opinions to the public or third parties, (3) requiring ten or more persons to maintain records, and (4) collecting information from federal agencies or employees for statistical purposes. It does not include the collection of information as part of criminal investigations, civil or administrative proceedings to which the government is a party, or intelligence activities.

Before an agency may engage in the collection of information, it must

1. undertake an internal review to evaluate the need for the information, describe the information to be collected, create a plan for its collection, and estimate the burden on private parties that the collection will impose;
2. publicly announce its reasons for collecting the information, the way in which the information will be used, the burden its collection will impose, whether responses are voluntary or mandatory, and the fact that in the absence of a valid control number a person is not bound to respond to any collection requirement;

3. submit the proposal for public notice and comment; and
4. submit the proposal and an accompanying justification to OIRA, which then seeks public comment on the agency's submission for 30 days.

If OIRA takes no action within 60 days, the proposed collection of information is deemed approved. In the case of a collection of information that is not part of or required by a rule that goes through notice and comment, OIRA may disapprove the collection if it determines that it is "unnecessary for any reason." In the case of a collection of information that is part of or required by a rule that goes through notice and comment, OIRA must submit comments as part of that proceeding and may disapprove the collection of information only if the agency's response to OIRA's comments was unreasonable. An independent regulatory commission may override an OIRA disapproval by majority vote. The Paperwork Reduction Act states that OIRA's approval of (or failure to act on) a proposed collection of information is not subject to judicial review, but it is silent about judicial review of disapprovals. Presumably, persons adversely affected by a disapproval can obtain judicial review under the APA, subject to standard requirements for judicial review. There is authority for persons to challenge agency actions arising from an OIRA disapproval.

When OIRA approves a collection of information, it assigns a control number to the collection. No one is subject to any penalty for failing to comply with an agency's collection of information requirement that does not display a valid control number. The absence of a valid control number, however, is no defense to a penalty for filing false information or for failing to file information required to be filed by statute.

B. Government Performance and Results Act

The Government Performance and Results Act of 1993, as amended by the GPRA Modernization Act of 2010, requires agencies to prepare a strategic plan and a performance plan annually, and to post these plans on the agency's website and notify the President and Congress of their availability.

The strategic plan must include a mission statement, a general statement of goals, a description of how those goals are to be achieved, a description of obstacles to their achievement, and a description of how the agency's performance goals contribute to its strategic goals, among other statements. The performance plan must establish performance goals; express those goals in objective, quantifiable, and measurable form (unless the director of OMB determines it is not feasible to do so); describe how those goals contribute to the agency's strategic plan and the federal government's performance goals; identify how those goals are to be achieved; provide a basis for measuring the agency's performance; and identify low-priority activities, among other statements.

The agency head must also make available updates on performance, comparing actual performance achievements with the agency's performance goals, not less than 150 days after the end of the fiscal year, and more frequently if it can do so at a reasonable level of administrative burden. These updates must provide a detailed review and assessment of the agency's successes and failures in achieving its performance goals. OMB must make an annual determination of whether the agency met its performance goals, and report on unmet goals to the head of the agency, the Senate Committee on Homeland Security and Governmental Affairs, the House Committee on Oversight and Governmental Reform (now Oversight and Accountability), and the GAO. If the agency's activities have not met its performance goals as determined by OMB for one fiscal year, the agency must designate a senior official to oversee its performance improvement and must submit a performance improvement plan to OMB. If OMB determines the agency's activities have not met its performance goals for two consecutive years, the agency head must submit to Congress a description of the actions the administration will take to improve performance, and describe any additional funding the agency will obligate to achieve the goal. If OMB determines the agency has not met its performance goals for three consecutive fiscal years, OMB shall submit recommendations to Congress on actions to improve the agency's performance, including reauthorization proposals, statutory changes, and planned executive actions.

The director of OMB must coordinate with agencies to improve the performance of the federal government and to establish priority goals, and every two years, or as otherwise determined by the director of OMB, the head of each agency shall identify a set of priority goals.

C. Regulatory Flexibility Act

The Regulatory Flexibility Act of 1980, 5 U.S.C. §§ 601–612, requires agencies to consider the special needs and concerns of small entities in the regulatory process. Small entities include small businesses as defined in the Small Business Act, 15 U.S.C. §§ 631, *et seq.*; not-for-profit organizations that are not dominant in their field; and governmental jurisdictions with a population of less than 50,000.

1. *Unified Agenda*

In October and April of each year, each agency must publish a "regulatory flexibility agenda" in the *Federal Register* that identifies and describes all rules under consideration that are likely to have a significant economic impact on a substantial number of small entities. The agenda must be submitted to the chief counsel for advocacy of the Small Business Administration (SBA) for comment.

2. *Regulatory Flexibility Analysis*

When proposing a regulation subject to notice-and-comment requirements, whether under the APA or any other law, an agency must make available for public comment an initial regulatory flexibility analysis (IRFA), unless the agency head certifies that the proposed rule will not have a significant economic impact on a substantial number of small entities. Courts have interpreted the significant economic impact as being limited to the direct cost effects of having to comply with a regulation and not including the indirect economic effects on small entities that may result from a regulation. The IRFA must be submitted to the chief counsel for advocacy of the SBA, and either a copy of the IRFA or a summary must be published in the *Federal Register*. An IRFA must contain a description of the reasons why the agency is considering the rule, a statement of the objectives of and legal basis for the rule, a description of and (where feasible) an estimate of the number of small entities to which the rule will apply, a description of any reporting or recordkeeping requirements contained in the rule, an identification of other federal rules that may duplicate or overlap with the rule, and a description of significant alternatives to the rule that would accomplish the stated objectives while minimizing economic effects on small entities. The Consumer Financial Protection Bureau (CFPB) must also include a discussion of those alternatives, a description of any increase in the cost of credit for small entities resulting from the proposed rule, a description of alternatives to the proposed rule that accomplish the stated objections of applicable statutes and minimize any increase in the cost of credit for small entities, and advice for small entities regarding impacts of the proposed rule on the cost of credit.

In the case of rules issued by the CFPB, Environmental Protection Agency, or the Occupational Safety and Health Administration, the agency must, prior to publication of the IRFA, notify the chief counsel for advocacy of the potential impacts of the proposed rule on small entities, so that he or she may identify representatives of the likely affected small entities for their advice and recommendations about the potential impacts. Unless this requirement is waived by the chief counsel for advocacy, these agencies must then convene a "review panel" consisting of employees from the agency, OIRA, and the chief counsel's office to review the proposed regulation, any other material developed in connection with the proposed rule, and the comments of the small-entity representatives. Within 60 days, the review panel must publicly report on the comments and its findings on the issues discussed in the IRFA. Other agencies *may* in their discretion also utilize this procedure if they wish.

Unless the agency head certifies that the final rule will not have a significant economic impact on a substantial number of small entities, it must be published with a final regulatory flexibility analysis (FRFA). The FRFA must contain a statement of the need for and objectives of the rule; a statement of and response to significant issues raised by the comments received (including, in particular, those of the chief counsel for advocacy of the SBA); a description of the small entities to which the rule will apply and an estimate of their number; a description of any reporting or recordkeeping requirements; a description of the steps the agency has taken to minimize the economic impact on small entities, including a statement of the reasons for adopting the alternative selected and for not adopting other alternatives; and, in the case of the CFPB, a description of steps the agency has taken to minimize any additional cost of credit for small entities. If a rule is a response to an emergency, the head of an agency may delay the completion of the FRFA until not later than 180 days after the publication of the final rule. If the FRFA is not published within 180 days, the rule automatically lapses and has no effect.

Neither the chief counsel nor a review panel has authority to veto or reject an agency proposal or regulatory flexibility analysis. The chief counsel is required to report annually to the President and to relevant congressional committees on agency compliance with the act and is authorized to appear as amicus curiae in any action seeking judicial review of a rule.

3. *Periodic Review of Rules*

The Regulatory Flexibility Act also requires agencies to engage in a ten-year review cycle of their regulations that have a significant economic effect on a substantial number of small entities. Each year agencies are to publish in the *Federal Register* the list of such rules that are to be reviewed in the following 12 months.

4. *Judicial Review*

A small entity adversely affected or aggrieved by final agency action may obtain judicial review under the APA of an agency's compliance with the requirements applicable to FRFAs, the validity of any certification that a rule will not have a significant economic effect on a substantial number of small entities, and an agency's compliance with the requirement for periodic review of its rules. The act establishes a maximum statute of limitations for such actions at one year from the date of the final agency action. The act allows a court, in addition to or in lieu of its other remedial powers under the APA, to defer the enforcement of a rule against small entities.

D. Attorney General Supervision of Litigation

By statute, the Department of Justice authorizes and handles most litigation involving agencies, including both enforcement actions that an agency wishes to bring and challenges to agency action under the APA. Even where an agency does have independent litigating authority, the attorney general and the solicitor general, with rare exceptions, have the exclusive authority to pursue and conduct litigation in the Supreme Court on behalf of the agency. By controlling the agency's litigation, the Department of Justice is able to affect the manner in which agencies perform their statutory duties.

INDEX

M

N

O

P

R